FOREWORD BY DR.MARTIN TRENCH
CO-AUTHOR OF VI[illegible] ATOLOGY

THE ART OF REVELATION

DR.JONATHAN WELTON

The Art of Revelation
Jonathan Welton, Copyright © 2017

Welton Academy
P.O. Box 92126
Rochester, NY 14692
www.weltonacademy.com

Printed in the United States
ISBN 978-0-9905752-6-9

CONTENTS

PART ONE
Revelation as a Masterful Painting

Viewing the Painting - 11
Building the Picture Frame - 17
Naming the Work - 37
Examining the Structure of the Story - 45

PART TWO
The Nine Major Components

The Introduction - 61
Vision 1: The Seven Churches - 67
Vision 2: The Seven Seals - 77
Vision 3: The Seven Trumpets - 85
Vision 4: Followers of the Lamb or the Beast - 103
Vision 5: The Seven Bowls of Wrath - 115
Vision 6: The Babylonian Harlot - 121
Vision 7: The Millennium, New Heavens, and New Earth - 131
The Epilogue -149

CONCLUSION
Is Revelation Still Relevant?

FOREWORD

BY DR. MARTIN TRENCH

Imagine you are walking around an art gallery, looking at various paintings. You know a little bit about art, but you are by no means an art expert. As you look at a painting, the main object in the painting impacts you. You notice other details in the background, but you are more acquainted with looking at common photographs than with looking at paintings, and background is usually just…well, background. It's the main subject that is important.

After making your way through most of the gallery, you notice an art expert who is taking a group on a tour around the gallery, and you decide to tag along. He stops at all the paintings you have just looked at, but he sees things in the painting that you missed. Turns out, the "background" in these paintings is not just a random background like it may be in a photo taken with your smart phone. The artist has taken time to choose what to put in the background and, as the expert explains, it all has meaning. He talks about the painter—where he lived at the time, what the political circumstances were, why he chose certain subjects, and what it was that he was seeking to communicate through the images he used. Suddenly, you find that the painting makes sense. It's not just a "nice picture"—but a story, a message. It has meaning.

As you mull this revelation over, you begin to feel a bit defensive about what you are learning. Why do you need to have an expert with a degree in art history to explain a painting to you? Is it true that you can't appreciate or understand a painting unless you find an expert to explain it to you? It sounds like a lot of highbrow intellectualism, and it's ruining your appreciation of art! You walk away and enter the gift shop that is always just before the exit. You browse for a while and see lots of books—not highbrow, overly intellectual books, but easy to read and highly informative books about many of the artists featured in the gallery. Suddenly, you realize that you don't need to find an art expert every time you want to understand a painting. Instead, you can become more educated about the artists and their art by studying a bit. You buy a few books, take them home, and read them. You feel like your understanding has been expanded. Now you not only see the skill of the artists, but you understand the messages they were seeking to communicate. You had been looking at art through the lens of your own culture, history, ideas, and experiences, and you had missed the point. Now you are able to see art from the perspective of the painter, and you see the artist's original intention. It's a real "aha" moment.

This is how many people react to the Book of Revelation. They read it and process it through their own culture and experiences (including Hollywood movies, poorly made Christian movies, and a lack of knowledge of ancient history). If an expert who has been studying Revelation in-depth for many years comes along and explains the history, culture, background, meaning, and fulfillment of the prophecies in Revelation, many people's first reaction is to dismiss it as theological intellectualism. "You mean I now have to find an expert to explain Revelation to me? The Holy Spirit isn't enough?" they say.

But the truth is, once we "see" something, we can never "unsee" it. Once someone has explained, for example, the history of Emperor Nero, how his own subjects called him "that great beast," and how he had statues to himself set up at the entrance to the market places in Asia Minor and insisted that no one be allowed to buy or sell without first offering worship to his statue—we can't forget that. Every time we read Revelation 13, that knowledge now comes flooding back, and no matter how much we want to believe the latest internet video about who the Beast of Revelation is, it no longer convinces us because our gullibility has been ruined. No, we don't have to find an expert. We can *"study to show yourself approved"* (2 Tim. 2:15) and become experts ourselves. The more we do this, the more we will have a hunger to dig and research and experience continual "aha" moments as the original intention of the Book of Revelation becomes clear.

Dr. Jonathan Welton is like the art expert in my illustration. He has studied Revelation and the historical background that it was written in for many years, in great depth, and from a wide range of perspectives. As you read this book, he will open your eyes to see things "in the background" that you have never seen before, and he will explain their meaning. It will create a hunger within you to do some of your own digging and research and become competent at reading the language of symbols. That's what Revelation is—it's an apocalypse. In today's Western culture, we think that word means a catastrophe or a dystopian future or the end of the world. What the word actually means is "an unveiling" or "a revealing," and it describes a particular genre of prophetic writing (which was very popular in Jewish and Christian circles from 100 BC–100 AD) in which prophecy is delivered in the language of symbols. The Book of Revelation is basically a series of symbolic pictures, and the symbols have real-world meanings. It's an art gallery of paintings that tell a story of the end of one covenant and the beginning of a new and better covenant.

Browse through these symbolic paintings. Take time to look deeply into the background, and let your eyes be opened, your mind expanded, and your faith soar. Many thanks to Dr. Jonathan Welton for being our guide through this incredible gallery.

DR. MARTIN TRENCH

gateway.ac

martintrench.com

PART ONE

REVELATION AS A MASTERFUL PAINTING

VIEWING THE PAINTING

I remember my first time in Paris with my wife. We went to all the typical tourist sights, including the famous art museum, the Louvre. The museum itself is a work of art, as it is a former palace of Napoleon Bonaparte. One piece of art stands out in my memory when I think of the Louvre. It was this massive painting of Napoleon on a horse visiting the battlefront. It is named "Napoleon on the battlefield of Eylau."[1] From floor to ceiling and wall to wall, this painting depicted the cold and brutal realities of death and war.

Let's imagine that we were standing together in front of the painting of Napoleon, but you had never heard of Napoleon. Suddenly you step extremely close to the painting. Pointing at one tiny blotch of color, you ask, "What is this patch of color? What does it mean? What does it represent?"

In response, I gently pull on your arm, guiding you back to the place where you can properly see the whole painting. "No," I say. "To understand the painting, you first need to step back, not forward. You must learn who Napoleon was, what wars were being fought, where they were fighting, and why."

---

[1] http://www.louvre.fr/en/oeuvre-notices/napoleon-battlefield-eylau

Like this painting, the Book of Revelation is a beautiful tapestry of images and symbols. In order to understand it, we first need to step back and look at the entire piece of art. We need to look at the big picture. Yet often people do exactly the opposite. Like you did in our imaginary scenario, they move too close to the painting and point at tiny patches of color, demanding isolated interpretations of those particles.

As one who would like to explain this painting, I ask that we start by standing back and taking in the painting at once, as a whole. Then I will tell you about the artist who painted it, why He painted it, and the historical context that surrounded this painter and influenced the way He created His painting. We need to understand these points surrounding the painting before we step closer to examine the details. If we don't do this first, our interpretation of it will be slanted by personal preference. Instead, we want our interpretation to be shaped by an understanding of what the artist intended. We are most likely to get this right if we look at the big picture first. Step one in getting the big picture in view is becoming familiar with the four main ways that people interpret Revelation.

FOUR VIEWS OF REVELATION

When approaching the Book of Revelation, people generally take one of four main methods for interpretation: idealism, futurism, historicism, and preterism.[2] Each of these methods of interpretation answers the basic four questions—*when, how, why*, and *where*—very differently.

---

[2] There are roughly three main camps within Preterism:

1. Kik Preterism, founded by Marcellus J. Kik, which teaches that most of Matthew 24 was fulfilled by AD 70. This camp does not recognize the Old Covenant to New Covenant shift that was taking place in the first century. cont pg. 13

To understand this, let's imagine four art experts standing in front of our large old painting called the Book of Revelation, and each expert has been trained by one of these four schools of thought. A passerby joins the group of experts and begins to ask the four important questions in hopes of understanding the painting.

He begins with the first question: *"When was this painting created?"*

The preterist responds first. "It was likely painted during the reign of Nero, based on the prophecy about seven kings listed in Revelation 17. It was painted regarding the AD 70 destruction of Jerusalem, and as a prophecy of that event, it was written in advance of that event."

Then the idealist, futurist, and historicist chime in together. "It doesn't really matter when it was painted," they say, "because the content is prophetic. It is probably about distant events and mysterious symbols.

The novice then introduces his second question, *"How was the painting painted?"* he asks. *"What medium did the artist use?"*

Once again, the preterist quickly speaks, saying, "Revelation was painted in the same manner as the books of Ezekiel, Jeremiah, and Isaiah, which all describe the first destruction of Jerusalem in 586 BC. John chose this style because it would

---

2. Partial Preterism, which is the largest contingent of preterists. They maintain that the destruction of Jerusalem in AD 70 was in large part a shifting from the Old Covenant to the New Covenant. Also they hold that most prophecy in the New Testament has been fulfilled, but that Jesus will have a final return in our future.

3. Full Preterism, a small group which believes that all New Testament prophecy has been fulfilled, including Jesus' final return. In recent years, this fringe group has grown rapidly by means of social media presence.

I will only be referring to Partial Preterism in the content of this book.

have clearly shown his audience that it was about the forthcoming second destruction of Jerusalem in AD 70."

The other three nodded in mild agreement, and then voice their differences. "We do agree that Revelation is full of Old Testament symbolism and imagery, yet we definitely do not agree that John painted it this way because of the AD 70 destruction."

The idealist adds, "John chose these symbols to point to the ongoing spiritual cosmic struggle between the kingdom of darkness and the kingdom of light, in which light ultimately wins."

"I'd say, instead, that he cloaked all of church history in mysterious symbolism centuries before it would unfold as it has and continues to unfold," the historicist says.

Finally, the futurist adds his point of view. "I agree that there are symbols and Old Testament references, but I believe that it will all make sense someday in the future when these events begin."

"All this is very interesting," the novice says. *"But, why did the artist paint this painting?"*

This time, the historicist chimes in first. "John was compelled to paint all of human history into one work of art. He painted it in advance of all the major coming events, centuries ahead of time. This has always been the nature of prophecy."

The futurist shook his head, saying, "I believe John was transported in a vision to the distant future, and when he returned from his vision, he painted all that he witnessed about the time of the end of human history."

After quietly thinking for a few moments, the idealist says, "I disagree with you both. John was a very mystical man. We see this from his strange Gospel account, which is so very different from the other three. I believe John wanted to show the cosmic struggle and the victory of Jesus in grand splendor."

At last, the preterist speaks. "I keep telling you guys, the early church was surviving under brutal persecution, and in that context, John said his painting was understandable (Rev. 13:18) and a blessing (Rev. 1:3; 22:7) to those who saw it. If his painting was about the distant future or served as an overlay of church history, how would this encourage them? I believe the Christians in the first century knew exactly what John's painting meant."

"OK. I can see the four of you don't agree on much," says the novice, chuckling. "Perhaps you can give me an answer to my final question: *Where was the painting painted? What location does it reference?"*

"The painting," says the idealist, "represents the heavenlies and is painted with all the spiritual pictures and components expected of a story about the battle between light and darkness."

"I disagree," says the futurist. "The location referred to in the painting is the planet earth in the future."

The historicist then adds his perspective. "The location isn't so important, considering that this has been unfolding and will continue to unfold over time. Although the city with seven hills is probably Rome, (Rev. 17:9) and Babylon the Harlot is probably the Roman Catholic Church."

The preterist answers last, saying, "The numbers, dimensions, measurements, and specifics that are recorded in the painting all made perfect sense to first-century Christians. There was very little mystery to the imagery that John used to convey his message to his intended audience. Only as the dust of church history has settled has this painting become more mysterious."

The other three stare in disbelief at the preterist, who always seemed to be proposing the most unusual ideas. Our bystander novice smiles and thanks his expert friends. "Clearly," he says, "there are four different ways to look at this painting. Now I will have to decide which one I like the best."

This imaginary dialogue gives us a basic understanding of each of these viewpoints. In the next chapter, we will examine the answers to the bystander's four important questions more closely. These questions are the key to helping us see the big picture of Revelation.

BUILDING THE PICTURE FRAME

To arrive at a biblically and historically accurate view of this most important painting, we must find out the original intentions of the artist and how his original audience would have received it. In other words, we need to know what exactly the Holy Spirit was saying when He wrote the Book of Revelation and how the early believers would have interpreted it. To understand its application to us, these many years later, we must first understand how it applied to the first century Christians. This is the big picture we are seeking, and it is encapsulated in the answers to our four important questions—*when, how, why,* and *where*. The answers to these questions are the frame for this painting.

1. WHEN WAS THIS PAINTING CREATED?

When we look at a painting of a battle scene, if we want to understand what was happening, we need to know when the painting was painted and what time and event it was about. Without that understanding, it would be impossible for us to understand many of the details of the painting specific to that period and event. Are we looking at a painting of World War I or World War II? Perhaps it is of the American Civil War or the

American Revolutionary War. Knowing the date of the painting will help us determine which events are being depicted.

In the same way, it is crucial to understand when the Book of Revelation was written. There are two main positions on the dating of Revelation. One camp says it was written around AD 65, just prior to the AD 70 destruction of Jerusalem. The other camp places it later, in AD 96, twenty-six years after Jerusalem's fall. The modern and popular position has, for the most part, been the later date. Yet, most of the evidence within Scripture indicates the book was written before the fall of Jerusalem. The reason that modern teachers point to a later date is because the leader of Rome in AD 96 was Domitian, and the Church historian, Irenaeus, writing around AD 120, seemed to say that Revelation was written during Domitian's reign.[3] Yet for many historians, Irenaeus has a credibility problem, because he also wrote that Jesus was in ministry from the age of thirty to the age of fifty (instead of three and a half years).[4] That mistake on his part has caused people to question his reliability with dates and numbers. But let's assume for a moment that Irenaeus was correct and that John was on Patmos during the reign of Domitian.

With that assumption, the next question we need to ask is, "Which reign of Domitian?" Frank Viola points out a little known but crucial fact in his book, *The Untold Story of the New Testament Church*. Domitian was emperor for a six-month period in AD 70; then he was again emperor from AD 81–96.[5] This means that, even if Irenaeus wrote accurately, he could have been referring to this earlier time period, which was prior to the fall of Jerusalem. The point is, the evidence from Irenaeus that

---

[3] Kenneth Gentry, *Before Jerusalem Fell*, (Braselton, GA: American Vision, 1998), 45–67.

[4] Ibid., 63–64.

[5] Viola, *The Untold Story of the New Testament Church* (Shippensburg, PA: Destiny Image, 2005), 176.

is used to prove a later date is not at all conclusive. So, leaving aside the debate over Irenaeus, let's look, instead, at the text of Revelation itself, which I believe offers us nine solid proofs that Revelation was written prior to AD 70.[6]

Proof #1: *The Syriac*

The first proof for an earlier dating of Revelation is the witness of one of the most ancient versions of the New Testament, called *The Syriac*. The title page of the fourth-century Syriac Version, called the *Peshitto*, says this:

> Again the revelation, which was upon the holy John the Evangelist from God when he was on the island of Patmos where he was thrown by the emperor Nero.

Nero Caesar ruled over the Roman Empire from AD 54 to AD 68. This means John had to have been on the island of Patmos during this earlier time period. One of the oldest versions of the Bible tells us that Revelation was written before AD 70! This alone is a very compelling argument.

Proof #2: Revelation 17:10

Second, when we look at the internal evidence, we find a very clear indicator of the date of authorship in Revelation 17:10: *"They are also seven kings. Five have fallen, one is, the other has not yet come; but when he does come, he must remain for only a little while."* This passage, which speaks of the line of rulers in Rome, tells us exactly how many rulers had already come, which one

[6] *Before Jerusalem Fell*, by Dr. Kenneth Gentry, is an important book on this subject. In it, Gentry, the leading preterist scholar on the Book of Revelation, examines the internal and external evidence for dating Revelation prior to AD 70. Another helpful book is John A. T. Robinson's *Re-dating the New Testament*, in which he concludes that the entire New Testament was written before AD 70.

was currently in power, and that the next one would only last a short while. This accurately identifies the rule of Nero and gives an outline of the Roman Empire of the first century. The succession of the first seven Roman Emperors went like this:

"Five have fallen..."

Julius Caesar (49–44 BC)

Augustus (27 BC–AD 14)

Tiberius (AD 14–37)

Caligula (AD 37–41)

Claudius (AD 41–54)

"One is..."

Nero (AD 54–68)

"the other has not yet come; but when he does come, he must remain for only a little while."

Galba (June AD 68–January AD 69, a six-month rule)

Of the first seven kings, five had come (Julius Caesar, Augustus, Tiberius, Gaius, and Claudius), one was currently in power (Nero), and one had not yet come (Galba), but would only remain for a short time (six months). From this we can clearly see that the current Caesar at the time of John's writing was the sixth Caesar, Nero.

Proof # 3: Those Who Pierced Him

Our third proof is found in the Hebrew idiom "coming on clouds,"[7] which speaks of God coming to bring judgment on a

[7] The phrase coming on clouds is used in Ezekiel, Jeremiah, and Isaiah in reference to God coming in judgment on a city or a nation. Whether it was Babylon or Edom or Egypt or Israel, this idiom meant He was coming to bring judgment. This was commonly understood prophetic language, and it does not speak of the end of the world. I cover this more fully in my book *Raptureless, 3rd edition*, pages 103–105.

city or nation. That is what Jesus came to do in AD 70. Revelation 1:7 tells us the target of God's judgment:

> *Lo, he doth come with the clouds, and see him shall every eye, even* ***those who did pierce him,*** *and wail because of him shall* ***all the tribes of the land.*** *Yes! Amen* (Revelation 1:7 YLT).

Here, the phrase *"those who did pierce him"* refers to the people of the first century. At any later time in history, these people would be deceased. Yet, according to this passage, they were expected to be alive at the time of this verse's fulfillment. This tells us that the prophecy of Revelation 1:7 had to be fulfilled within a short time after Jesus' death, while His accusers were still alive on earth. In other words, it was fulfilled in the destruction of Jerusalem that happened in AD 70. For this to be true, the Book of Revelation must have been written before AD 70.

Proof #4: Influence of the Jews and Judaizing Heretics

Our fourth proof is found in the fact that the activity of the Jewish leaders and Judaizers in the Church is mentioned in the letters to the churches in Revelation. Jesus speaks of *"those who say they are Jews and are not, but are a synagogue of Satan"* (Rev. 2:9). This was a clear reference to the Jewish leaders who persecuted the Christians. Also, among the Christians existed a group called the Judiazers, who tried to turn Christians back to the old covenant Jewish Law. This was a major heresy in the first century church, and Paul wrote quite a bit against it. Prior to AD 70, both the Jewish leaders outside the church and the Judiazers within the church had a strong negative impact upon believers. About them, Jesus says:

> *I will make those who are of the synagogue of Satan, who claim to be Jews though they are not, but are liars—I will make them*

> *come and fall down at your feet and acknowledge that I have loved you* (Revelation 3:9).

Before the AD 70 destruction, it was advantageous to be a Jew. The Jewish people had a favored relationship with Rome. They were allowed to have their own police force and follow their own Temple system, so long as they continued in subservience to the empire. But all that changed in AD 70, when the Roman army destroyed Jerusalem and killed more than a million Jews. Ever since that time, history has not been particularly kind to the Jewish people, and I think it is safe to say that after AD 70 people were not touting their status as Jews. These verses about people who falsely claimed to be Jews only makes sense in the pre–AD 70 context. Since the destruction of Jerusalem in AD 70, it has not been advantageous to claim to be Jewish.

In this way, these verses point to an earlier dating of the letter. The first century Jews and Judaizers lost a great deal of influence after the destruction of AD 70, because the Jewish religious system had been destroyed and the Jewish population significantly diminished. Only if we give the Book of Revelation an early date of authorship does the significant presence and threat of the Jews and Judiazers make sense.

Proof #5: Existence of Jerusalem and the Temple

Along the same lines, the fifth proof of an earlier date is the existence and integrity of Jerusalem and the Temple in Revelation 11. This suggests that the book was written before the destruction of AD 70. On the other hand, if the Book of Revelation was in fact written in AD 96, only twenty-six years after the destruction of the Temple and the Holy City, it is shocking that John didn't mention the recent massacre of the city and Temple. The sheer unlikeliness that John would omit such a crucial piece of

Jewish history tells us that the book must have been written prior to AD 70.

Proof # 6: Time-related Passages

Our sixth proof is in the time-related passages at both the beginning and end of Revelation. In Revelation 1:1 and 1:3, as well as 22:10 and 22:20, we find internal time indicators that declare *"the time is near,"* it is *"shortly to come to pass," "he is coming quickly,"* and *"behold, he comes speedily."* John clearly wrote that the time of judgment was close. This only fits if the book was written before the destruction of Jerusalem.

Proof # 7: John's Appearance in AD 96

A seventh reason to believe the Book of Revelation was written at the earlier date is the appearance of John in AD 96. Jerome noted in his writings that John was seen in AD 96, and he was so old and infirm that "he was with difficulty carried to the church, and could speak only a few words to the people."[8] We must put this fact together with Revelation 10:11, which says John must *"prophesy again concerning many peoples and nations and tongues and kings."* It is difficult to imagine John would be able to speak to many nations and many kings at any date after AD 96 since he was already elderly and feeble.

Proof # 8: Timetable Comparison with Daniel

Eighth, in Daniel's prophesy about events that would happen hundreds of years later, he was told to *"roll up and seal the words of the scroll until the time of the end,"* because it was a long way

[8] Harold Eberle and Martin Trench, *Victorious Eschatology* (Yakima, WA: Worldcast Publishing, 2006), 127.

off (Dan. 12:4ff). By contrast, John was told, *"Do not seal up the words of the prophecy of this scroll, because the time is near"* (Rev. 22:10). While Daniel was told to seal the prophecy up because it was a long way off (about 500 years), John was told not to seal it up because it was about to come to pass. In other words, the prophetic events were closer than 500 years. This only makes sense if the book was written prior to AD 70 and the prophecy was fulfilled in AD 70.

Proof #9: Only Seven Churches

Our ninth proof for an early dating of the writing of Revelation is the existence of only seven churches in Asia Minor (see Rev. 1). This tells us that the book was written before the greater expansion of Christianity into that region, which occurred after the fall of Jerusalem.

These nine points strongly point to a dating of the writing of Revelation prior to AD 70. The debate continues in scholarly circles, yet I believe these points are convincing enough for us to move forward with the idea of a pre–AD 70 writing of Revelation.

This brings us to our next question, *How?*

2. HOW WAS THE PAINTING PAINTED? WHAT MEDIUM DID THE ARTIST USE?

Now that we have dated the creation of this masterpiece, we must also examine it within its larger context to understand the medium used and the backdrop on which it was created. Is it an oil painting? Or maybe it's a watercolor. Further, what style did the artist use? Every great painting is created as a statement within the larger context of the world of art. The great artists knew and appreciated one another's works, and in a sense, their works form a sort of conversation with one another on the issues of their day and the ideals of their art. No artwork is created in a vacuum. It is a part of its context, not just historically but also artistically. This is important, because it adds to the meaning and purpose of the medium and style of the painting. Artists do not make such choices haphazardly or randomly, and we should not understand them that way.

The same is true of the Book of Revelation. It was not written into an artistic or historical vacuum. It has for its context the entire Bible and the history of Israel from Abraham to Jesus. What this means is that strewn throughout Revelation are references to the bigger picture. It's imagery and style point backward, and to understand them, we need to understand what came before. That is a weak point for many of us, because most modern Christians are not well acquainted with Old Testament history or prophecy. This is exactly why Revelation seems so daunting to us.

We struggle to understand the Book of Revelation because we struggle to understand the history of the Old Testament. If I asked a well-studied Christian to sketch out a rough timeline of the Old Testament, it would look something like this:

- Adam and Eve (the Garden of Eden)
- Noah (the Flood)
- Abraham
- Isaac
- Jacob
- Joseph
- Egyptian slavery
- Moses (the Exodus)

- Joshua
- the Judges
- King Saul
- King David
- King Solomon

This rough timeline is accurate, but it is incomplete. We know the history of Israel does not end with Solomon, yet after Solomon the story gets too complicated for many modern believers. As a result, many of us never get a handle on the Old Testament past the reign of King Solomon. For the average Bible reader, the timeline breaks down after Solomon into a jumble of major and minor prophets, a divided kingdom, Elijah and Elisha, the exile to Babylon, and the return to rebuild Jerusalem. For many of us, this whole section of texts feels troublesome and challenging to relate to or understand. However, to understand the Book of Revelation we must *especially* understand the Old Testament after Solomon.

For that reason, here we will iron out (at least a little bit) the timeline after Solomon.

- After Solomon dies, Israel divides into two kingdoms, which spiritually and morally enter into drastic decline. Many evil rulers come and go in both kingdoms.
- Elijah and Elisha fight against the tide of wickedness flooding into the divided kingdom.
- Isaiah, Ezekiel, and Jeremiah prophesy a coming destruction upon Jerusalem for her wickedness.
- Babylon brings destruction upon the kingdom of Judah and takes Daniel and others as captives. Assyria destroys

the Northern Kingdom, whose ten tribes are now essentially lost to history.

- Daniel writes the Book of Daniel while in Babylonian captivity.
- Esther protects her people from destruction while still in captivity.
- Finally, the exile in Babylon ends, and the Israelites return to Jerusalem. They rebuild the city and the Temple under Ezra and Nehemiah.
- Interspersed in the story from Solomon to Ezra and Nehemiah are the smaller books of the minor prophets.

The most important Old Testament book to a proper understanding of the Book of Revelation is Ezekiel. Ezekiel prophesied the destruction of Jerusalem in the Old Testament. This was fulfilled when Babylon invaded the city, destroyed the Temple, and took many people into captivity. Though the prophecy of Ezekiel was already fulfilled in the past, it is important for us to understand, because the Book of Revelation is in many ways modeled after the Book of Ezekiel. This makes sense, since the destruction John prophesied in Revelation was similar to the previous destruction prophesied by Ezekiel. In the big picture context of Jewish history, modeling Revelation after Ezekiel would have spoken volumes to John's Jewish contemporaries.

They would have taken note of the extensive parallels between the prophecy of Revelation and the prophecy of Ezekiel:

1. The Throne Vision (Rev. 4; Ezek. 1)
2. The Book (Rev. 5; Ezek. 2–3)
3. The Four Plagues (Rev. 6:1–8; Ezek. 5)
4. The Slain under the Altar (Rev. 6:9–11; Ezek. 6)

5. The Wrath of God (Rev. 6:12–17; Ezek. 7)
6. The Seal on the Saint's Foreheads (Rev. 7; Ezek. 9)
7. The Coals from the Altar (Rev. 8; Ezek. 10)
8. No More Delay (Rev. 10:1–7; Ezek. 12)
9. The Eating of the Book (Rev. 10:8–11; Ezek. 2)
10. The Measuring of the Temple (Rev. 11:1–2; Ezek. 40–43)
11. Jerusalem and Sodom (Rev. 11:8; Ezek. 16)
12. The Cup of Wrath (Rev. 14; Ezek. 23)
13. The Vine of the Land (Rev. 14:18–20; Ezek. 15)
14. The Great Harlot (Rev. 17–18; Ezek. 16, 23)
15. The Lament over the City (Rev. 18; Ezek. 27)
16. The Scavengers' Feast (Rev. 19; Ezek. 39)
17. The First Resurrection (Rev. 20:4–6; Ezek. 37)
18. The Battle with Gog and Magog (Rev. 20:7–9; Ezek. 38–39)
19. The New Jerusalem (Rev. 21; Ezek. 40–48)
20. The River of Life (Rev. 22; Ezek. 47)

It is no accident that these books so closely parallel each other. John, guided by the Holy Spirit, was very intentional in how he presented his material—how he painted his painting. He chose his artistic medium with a specific audience in mind, and that audience would have understood the significance. Reading Revelation without an understanding of Ezekiel is like listening to the Weird Al Yankovic song, "Fat" without ever having heard Michael Jackson's song, "Bad." Because the second so closely imitates the first, it must be understood in the context of the first.

What many modern readers don't realize is that the Book of Ezekiel is the turning point of the Old Testament. Before Ezekiel, from Adam to Solomon, the kingdom of Israel continually gained momentum. This momentum began to slow with the divided kingdom, but Ezekiel brought any remaining momentum to a screeching halt. His prophecy was followed by captivity, exile, a post-exilic return to Jerusalem, and a painful rebuilding process while still under a measure of captivity. After four hundred years of silence, the story of the Jews is resumed in the New Testament with Jerusalem under Roman oppression. To model Revelation after Ezekiel meant prophesying a similar sort of destruction and decline for the Jews.

John's first-century readers would have not only recognized the parallel between these two books, but they would have also understood that John was prophesying a very similar event to what Ezekiel had prophesied. The only difference was the destroyer (Rome instead of Babylon) and the end result. While Ezekiel prophesied a post-exilic return and a rebuilding of Jerusalem, John did not prophesy either. Instead, he prophesied Jerusalem being replaced by a new heaven, new earth, and new (heavenly) Jerusalem. The early readers would have picked up on this difference, too, and the significant shift being prophesied.

The reality of this parallel is confirmed by the historical fact that the destruction of Jerusalem in 586 BC and the destruction of the temple in AD 70 happened on the same day in the Jewish calendar—the ninth day of Av. The incredible parallel in those two dates and the prophetic irony confirm that these two prophecies contain the same concept—except this time there will be no rebuilding and restoring. Instead of returning to the old covenant, they would transition completely into the new covenant. This is why John wrote the way he did. By using the same structure and imagery as Ezekiel, while also referring to the prophecies of Isaiah and Jeremiah, he painted a clear comparison between what had happened before and what was about to happen again.

- Ezekiel prophesied the destruction of Jerusalem in 586 BC.
- John prophesied the destruction of Jerusalem in AD 70.
- Ezekiel prophesied the post-exilic return and rebuilding of Jerusalem (see Ezek. 34–37).
- John prophesied no such return and no rebuilding of Jerusalem.

Ezekiel is to the Old Testament what the Book of Revelation is to the New Testament. Understanding this artistic medium that John used will help us understand our third question—*Why?*

3. WHY DID THE ARTIST PAINT THIS PAINTING?

After considering the *when* and *how* of the artwork, we must then consider the *why*. All art is painted with a purpose. Sometimes that purpose is simply for the sake of beauty. At other times, artists have an agenda or message that they hope to convey through their artwork. This is their *why*. In the case of Revelation, we must ask why John chose to write this work and, similarly, why Jesus chose to give him this prophecy. After all, the basic content of the Book of Revelation, that judgment is coming soon, was not a new message. Jesus had already prophesied about the coming destruction in AD 70 in His Olivet Discourse, as recorded in Matthew 24, Luke 21, and Mark 13. The early believers already had these books, and they were already on the alert, watching for the beginning of these events so that they could avoid being caught in the destruction. Considering that, we must ask, what was John's purpose in writing the Book of Revelation thirty-five years later?

We can find an answer to this, first, in the fact that John's Gospel does not include a prophecy of AD 70 and the coming destruction. In a sense, then, the Book of Revelation is a parallel to the Olivet Discourse recorded in the other three Gospels. John was a sort of renegade, in that he did not write his Gospel like the other three gospel writers. He took a completely different approach and recorded risky stories (like Jesus' command to eat His flesh and drink His blood) that the other Gospels omit. It makes sense, then, that John would not write the normal Olivet Discourse but the highly symbolic Book of Revelation that paralleled the Old Testament prophets. This fits with John's personality as a writer much more than it would have for any of the other New Testament writers.

Second, when Jesus appeared to John and gave him a vision that paralleled the destruction of Jerusalem in the Old Testament, it also served as an update and encouragement to the Christians who had believed for the last thirty-five years that Jesus would bring judgment very soon (see Luke 18:6–8). Jesus wanted to give His Church a comforting update. He was reminding them to keep watch and encouraging them that His judgment against the old covenant (and their resulting deliverance from persecution) was just around the corner.

From AD 30–70, the Church suffered terrible persecution at the hands of the Jewish Temple leaders. The persecution then intensified in AD 64–68 under Nero, who made it his goal to completely annihilate Christianity. When John wrote Revelation, many of his peers, the leaders of the early Church, had been killed by the Romans. The Church seemed to be in a desperate spot. During this very difficult time, the Church needed encouragement from Jesus. They needed reassurance that He was still planning to come back and that the time was soon. This is just what Revelation gave them. It was a sort of last cry and reminder: "It is coming. Do not lose hope! Stand strong and persevere!" Throughout Revelation, God tells His followers to be patient because His justice, wrath, and vengeance against the old covenant system were coming very soon.

This is the *why* of Revelation. It was both John's parallel to the Olivet Discourse and Jesus' encouragement to the Christians of the first century to keep holding on. This leads us to our final question—*Where?*

4. WHERE WAS THE PAINTING PAINTED? WHAT LOCATION DOES IT REFERENCE?

The last question we must address to get the full background picture for the masterpiece of Revelation is the question of where it was created. To understand a painting, one must consider not only the time when the painting was created, but also the place where the painting was painted and the region it refers to. This gives us insight into the culture and events that surrounded the creation of the painting and informed its purpose. Was it painted in France during the French Revolution or in Colonial America during the American Revolution? Is it a modern piece, or was it upon the wall of a cave in ancient times?

TIME TEXTS

The question of where the painting was painted is, of course, connected to the question of when, as the culture and events of a place changes over the years. For that reason, we must first briefly revisit the topic of timing. Earlier, we established that the Book of Revelation was written before AD 68, during the reign of Nero. We also looked at the time-texts within the book, or the passages that indicate a sense of timing. We noted that Revelation was an unsealed book (see Rev. 22:10) because the events were soon to take place, whereas Daniel was a sealed book (see Dan. 12:4) because its contents were about events in the *then* distant future—five hundred years later. About the fulfillments of its prophecies, the Book of Revelation says:

- What must *shortly* take place (see Rev. 1:1)
- For the time is *near* (see Rev. 1:3)
- I am coming to you *quickly* (see Rev. 2:16)
- I am coming *quickly* (see Rev. 3:11)
- The third woe is coming *quickly* (see Rev. 11:14)
- The things which must *shortly* take place (see Rev. 22:6)
- Behold, I am coming *quickly* (see Rev. 22:7)
- For the time is *near* (see Rev. 22:10)
- Behold, I am coming *quickly* (see Rev. 22:12)
- Yes, I am coming *quickly* (see Rev. 22:20)

Each of these statements indicates that the prophecy of Revelation would be fulfilled in the near future. Yet many modern readers have dismissed these verses.

The scholar Dr. Gordon Fee explains what is missing, which is a principle of accurate biblical interpretation. He says, "A text cannot mean what it never could have meant to its author or his or her readers."[9] In other words, we cannot simply look at the texts that say *soon* and conclude it couldn't be so because it

[9] Gordon D. Fee and Douglas Stuart, *How to Read the Bible for All Its Worth* (Grand Rapids, MI: Zondervan, 2003), 74.

was written two thousand years ago and we haven't identified anything in history that fits what we think it should look like! This should not be. Instead, we must diligently treat the text with respect. Our ignorance of history gives us no allowance for such a conclusion.

The text says *soon*; therefore, we must look for a soon fulfillment that respects the text. We also must not do violence to the text by forcing it to fit into history. If it fits into history, it should fit beautifully and with such smoothness as to not violate the conscience in the least. I believe Revelation does just that—*if* we understand it in its proper location, which is not the entire globe but the small region of the world where it was created and where its original audience lived.

LOCATION

The modern reader has been trained to read Revelation as if it was written about a global catastrophe. Unfortunately, our English translations are careless with the details regarding location. For example, when Revelation writes about a third of the grass, a third of the trees, and a third of the earth (see Rev. 8), the modern reader imagines this on a global scale. Yet the original wording of the Greek manuscripts paints an extremely different picture. The Greek word often translated as "earth" or "world" would be better-translated "land." This word is one of two Greek words that are commonly translated as *earth* in the New Testament. *Kosmos* means "the whole planet,"[10] while *ge* means "a local, inhabited earth" or "the land of a particular nation."[11] This word *ge* is used sixty-seven times in Revelation,

[10] *Strong's Exhaustive Concordance*, Greek #2889.

[11] Ibid., Greek #1093.

clearly showing us that the book is about a local, inhabited region, not about the entire planet. By contrast, *kosmos* is used only three times in Revelation:

> *The seventh angel sounded his trumpet, and there were loud voices in heaven, which said: "The kingdom of the world* [kosmos] *has become the kingdom of our Lord and of his Messiah, and he will reign for ever and ever"* (Revelation 11:15).

> *All inhabitants of the earth* [ge] *will worship the beast—all whose names have not been written in the Lamb's book of life, the Lamb who was slain from the creation of the world* [kosmos] (Revelation 13:8).

> *The inhabitants of the earth whose names have not been written in the book of life from the creation of the world* [kosmos] *will be astonished when they see the beast, because it once was, now is not, and yet will come* (Revelation 17:8b).

Each of these verses uses *kosmos* in reference to the whole planet earth. The remainder of the Book of Revelation refers to the events of a local area. Obviously, there is a huge difference between saying a third of the grass and trees around Israel will be burned and saying a third of the grass and trees of the planet will be burned. When we think of the damage that armies do to the landscape, this number seems very logical in a regional context. And that is exactly what happened locally in the land of Israel. The apostle John often used this word, *kosmos,* in his other writings—a whopping fifty-seven times in his gospel and seventeen times in First John alone. Yet he chose not to use it much in Revelation because *he was not writing about a global event.* This is an incredibly important point!

From this simple study of these two Greek words often translated as *world,* we can see that the Book of Revelation was not written about a global catastrophe but a *local* catastrophe. The contents of the entire Book of Revelation refer to local (*ge*) events, not global (*kosmos*) events. This explains why other horrific events in history were not prophesied and recorded in the Bible. The Book of Revelation is about a local event that was specifically connected to the history of the new covenant. Other historic events, while important to humanity, were not related to the covenant transition, and therefore, they are not prophesied within the biblical canon. Revelation is included in the Bible because it tells the story of the destruction of the old covenant at a specific time and location in our past. Understanding this element—the where of our painting—is everything in understanding what it means.

NAMING THE WORK

Another important aspect of any painting is its name. The same is true of a book. The full name of Revelation is "The Revelation of Jesus Christ." It is not the book of revelations in general but the revelation of someone specific—Jesus Christ. This should cause us to ask some questions. First, why is this unique from the events of Jesus' life and death? Was He fully revealed in His birth, ministry, death, and resurrection? Or is a further revelation necessary? Second, if He still needed to be revealed, what was hiding Him?

The ideas in these questions may seem to contradict much of what we have learned in Christianity, but they actually fit well with the New Testament, which speaks in several places of an imminent revealing of Jesus Christ. For example, Peter wrote:

> *These have come so that the proven genuineness of your faith—of greater worth than gold, which perishes even though refined by fire—may result in praise, glory and honor* ***when Jesus Christ is revealed*** (1 Peter 1:7).

Just a little bit later, he repeated this idea when he said, "*Therefore, with minds that are alert and fully sober, set your hope on the grace to be brought to you* ***when Jesus Christ is revealed at his***

coming" (1 Pet. 1:13). As mentioned previously, coming is an idiom used throughout Scripture to refer to God *coming* in judgment. Peter was not talking about Jesus' final coming in this passage, but about Jesus' coming in destruction on Jerusalem. Too often we personalize what we read in the New Testament letters. We must remind ourselves that Peter was writing to real people that he knew in the first century, and he says to *them* "that the proven genuineness of *your* faith" and "grace to be brought to *you*." Peter was writing to them, not to us; therefore, the events he was predicting would have been expected in their lifetime.

Likewise, in Second Thessalonians 1:6–7, while addressing people under tremendous persecution, Paul wrote:

> *God is just: He will pay back trouble to those who trouble you and give relief to you who are troubled, and to us as well. This will happen* ***when the Lord Jesus is revealed from heaven*** *in blazing fire with his powerful angels.*

That is exactly what happened in AD 70, when the destruction of Jerusalem brought an end to those who were troubling them. The Jewish persecution of Christians stopped, and though the Romans did continue to persecute the Christians, the severity of it significantly decreased after the death of Nero in AD 68. All this happened as Paul said it would—"*...when the Lord Jesus is revealed.*" In his first letter to the Corinthians, Paul also wrote of his first century expectations, "*Therefore you do not lack any spiritual gift as you eagerly* ***wait for our Lord Jesus Christ to be revealed***" (1 Cor. 1:7). These are just a few examples of a topic that is a prominent theme in the New Testament. The early believers were waiting for the full revelation of Jesus in the near future, and they knew it was connected to the destruction of Jerusalem. So, when John named the Book of Revelation, he was clearly advertising it as a prophesy of the revealing of Jesus in judgment on Jerusalem. It was the event they had all been waiting for.

This is connected to the second question—What was hiding (or veiling) Jesus? The answer is in Second Corinthians 3, where Paul talks about the old covenant.

> *Now if the ministry that brought death, which was engraved in letters on stone, came with glory, so that the Israelites could not look steadily at the face of Moses because of its glory, transitory though it was, will not the ministry of the Spirit be even more glorious? If the ministry that brought condemnation was glorious, how much more glorious is the ministry that brings righteousness! For what was glorious has no glory now in comparison with the surpassing glory.* ***And if what was transitory came with glory, how much greater is the glory of that which lasts*** (2 Corinthians 3:7–11).

First, Paul establishes that the glory of the new covenant is far greater than the glory of the old covenant ever was. Based on this, Paul concludes:

> *Therefore, since we have such a hope, we are very bold. We are not like Moses, who would put a veil over his face to prevent the Israelites from seeing the end of what was passing away. But their minds were made dull,* ***for to this day the same veil remains when the old covenant is read. It has not been removed, because only in Christ is it taken away.*** *Even to this day* ***when Moses is read, a veil covers their hearts.*** *But whenever anyone turns to the Lord, the veil is taken away. Now the Lord is the Spirit, and where the Spirit of the Lord is, there is freedom. And we all,* ***who with unveiled faces*** *contemplate the Lord's glory, are being transformed into his image with ever-increasing glory, which comes from the Lord, who is the Spirit* (2 Corinthians 3:12–18).

In other words, it was the old covenant that veiled Jesus. It veiled Him when He was born. It veiled Him when He died. And it veiled Him when He was resurrected. It wasn't until the events of Revelation that the old covenant veil was ultimately taken away. What Revelation prophesied became reality when the Temple and the old covenant were finally destroyed. The veil of judgment and death, through which people had seen God since the days of the Mosaic covenant, was finally removed. The old covenant had prevented people from seeing who God really is; all they had seen was judgment and condemnation. But in the destruction of AD 70, that veil was taken away, and we are now free to see God as the loving Father He is. The first century believers would have clearly understood that this is what Revelation is about—prophesying the destruction of the old covenant, which had been veiling God. Through destroying the old covenant, God would fully reveal the glory of Christ and His new covenant.

Knowing this helps us understand God's heart in the events of Revelation.

GOD'S HEART IN REVELATION

When people read Revelation without understanding the background and purpose, it can seem very terrifying, disturbing, tragic, and confusing. Many live with a fearful expectation of these events in their lifetime. Instead, we should actually be looking over our shoulder at these historically fulfilled prophecies with awe at their fulfillment and horror at their devastation. When we view Revelation with an understanding of the new covenant, we can begin to see God's heart in it. Certainly, the loss of life was tragic and terrible. We do not want to overlook that. However, to God, the events of the Book of Revelation were glorious and beautiful *because* they finally removed the veil of the old covenant that had disguised God's true heart.

God had suffered through fifteen hundred years of being misunderstood and rejected. The old covenant had veiled who God really was. This wasn't His idea, but Israel's. They had rejected His covenant offer to make them into a nation of priests, and instead, they had asked for the Law (the old covenant) and for a mediator (Moses) between them and God.[12] He wanted to speak with each of them, face-to-face, but they feared Him, so they asked for rules instead. However, when the old covenant system was destroyed in AD 70, the veil that hid God's nature was also destroyed. It could no longer get in the way and prevent people from relating with Him. If we get this, we can see how glorious the events of Revelation truly were.

Revelation was not about the destruction of a people but about the destruction of a flawed system that had veiled God for years. It was also the revelation (or unveiling) of the new covenant in Christ. We see this in Revelation 11:19, where it says:

> *Then God's temple in heaven was opened, and within his temple was seen the ark of his covenant. And there came flashes of lightning, rumblings, peals of thunder, an earthquake and a severe hailstorm.*

The earthly ark of the covenant had been lost in the destruction of Jerusalem in 586 BC. It had not been seen on earth for many years. When Jesus died, the Temple was shaken and the veil was torn, revealing an empty room where the ark should have been. When John saw the ark of the covenant in his vision, he was not seeing that old earthly ark of the old covenant, which

[12] See Exodus 19:3–6, Deuteronomy 5:23–27. For more information, see my book *Understanding the Whole Bible.*

had been lost. He was, instead, seeing the Temple in Heaven, where Jesus had entered and sprinkled His blood on the heavenly ark of the covenant (see Heb. 9:21–24). If Jesus had put His blood on the ark of the old covenant, His blood would have sealed us into the old covenant forever. Thankfully, instead, He put His blood on the ark of the new covenant in the Temple in Heaven. This was an incredible and glorious transition from the burden of the Law into the freedom of faith!

We see confirmation of Revelation as a covenant document in this often-misunderstood passage:

> *I warn everyone who hears the words of the prophecy of this scroll: If anyone adds anything to them, God will add to that person the plagues described in this scroll. And if anyone takes words away from this scroll of prophecy, God will take away from that person any share in the tree of life and in the Holy City, which are described in this scroll* (Revelation 22:18–19).

This command not to add to or take away from is found one other place in Scripture, in Deuteronomy 4:2, which says, *"Do not add to what I command you and do not subtract from it, but keep the commands of the Lord your God that I give you."* Here, it referenced the old covenant Law. Phrases like this were commonly used to seal covenants between two parties.[13] In Deuteronomy, it was the old covenant that was being sealed. In Revelation, the presence of these words should clue us into the fact that God was sealing His new covenant.

In this context, it makes absolute sense that a statement like this would close out the final book in the new covenant. The purpose of Revelation 22:18–19 is not to scare people but to demonstrate Revelation's position within the canon of the

[13] Meredith Kline, *The Treaty of the Great King* (Eugene, OR: Wipf and Stock, 2012), 59.

new covenant. It was another way of revealing that the whole book is a covenant book. As such, it was very important to the first century believers, who were relying on its instructions to be able to escape the coming destruction of Jerusalem. They needed the book to stay intact so that they would know what to do when they saw Jerusalem surrounded, and they needed it intact because it revealed the new covenant and the glory of Jesus. John named the book *The Revelation of Jesus Christ* to underscore this message. The events he prophesied were coming soon, and they would finally unveil the true nature of the Godhead. At long last, the true heart of God would be made manifest to the world, and the glory of the new covenant would begin to reshape the hearts and minds of people as they entered into the joy of His Kingdom.

EXAMINING THE STRUCTURE OF THE STORY

One of the biggest errors that almost all modern readers of Revelation make is to think that the book is written in a linear manner. If we try to read this ancient Hebrew text without knowing how to study ancient literature, it is easy to misinterpret the text and conclude that it is written about a sequence of events (12345), whether they are events in the past or the future. Yet to the one who understands ancient Hebrew texts, the events of Revelation unfold in a different pattern, which is based on the Hebrew prose contained in the book (123-4-321).

When we read the Bible, most of us do not think about the structure or form of the writing. We are very used to writing that does not have a particular form to it. However, for most of history, *poetry* was the major form of writing. This included spiritual and historical texts, not just what we think of as poetry today. In fact, much of the Bible is written in a form of Hebrew poetry called the chiastic arch or Hebrew ring composition. Though this structure is used throughout the Bible, many of us have not noticed it simply because we are unfamiliar with it. If we don't know that such a thing exists, the likelihood of us noticing it in a passage is very small, but once we learn about the structure, we begin to see that it is, in fact, utilized in very many places. The chiastic arch structure is one of the primary forms of Hebrew poetry, and it lends a specific emphasis to the text that often draws out subtle meanings.

The chiastic arch follows this pattern:

A

B

C

D

C

B

A

Instead of dividing the verses or ideas in a linear fashion, as we typically do in English, many Hebrew poems follow this cyclical arch form in which the first three parts (A, B, C) progress together toward a central idea (D). The final three parts (C, B, A) progress together back toward the original idea, bringing the poem full circle. Some chiasms are longer, and some are shorter, but the basic form stays the same regardless of length. The text is split in half, with the central idea being the longest and most important. The corresponding parts (A and A), while not usually identical, are similar and often help to explain each other. This pattern of repetition brings clarification and emphasis to the meaning of the poem.

Once we understand and recognize chiastic arches, the nuances of this form brings added depth and meaning to many passages in the Bible, including the Book of Revelation, which is in the form of a giant chiastic arch.

CHIASM IN REVELATION

The basic structure of Revelation can be outlined like this:

A – Greeting

B – Seven Churches

C – Seven Seals

D – Seven Trumpets, Angel, Two Witnesses

E – Woman, Dragon, Male Child

D – Two Beasts, Angel, Seven Bowls

C – Destruction of Babylon

B – Bride

A – Epilogue

At the beginning and end (A) are the greeting and the epilogue. The first B is the seven churches, and the second is the New Jerusalem and the Bride. Both of these are the Church, but there is a progression that happens from the state of the seven churches in part one to the Bride of Christ, who surfaces in part two after the marriage supper of the Lamb. The first C is the seven seals, and the second is the destruction of Babylon. The D on the first side is the seven trumpets, an angel, and the two witnesses. Then, the D on the other side is the two beasts, an angel, and the seven bowls. The parallelism of this structure is striking. In the middle (E)—the central event—we find the woman, the dragon, and the male child.

This central event (in Revelation 12) is the most important point, the centerpiece of the book.[14] It is the story of the incarna-

[14] It is commonly accepted that Revelation is a chiastic arch. The only debate is over how to divide it up. Mark Wilson's *The Seven Victor Sayings of Revelation* covers the different versions of a chiastic arch in Revelation. In most cases, commentators agree that chapter 12 is the centerpiece.

tion. The woman is a picture of the remnant of Israel (the true followers of God),[15] and she gives birth to a male child who *"will rule all the nations with an iron scepter"* (Rev. 12:5; see Ps. 2:9). This child is the covenant promised child—Jesus. The red dragon, who is at war with the child and with Michael the archangel, is the accuser of the brethren, Satan. When he is defeated and cast out of Heaven, he begins to fight against the woman's other children. These children who come after the firstborn, Jesus, are the early Christians, the true Israel (see Rom. 9:6–8).

In Revelation 12, we get the whole picture of the gospel and the story of the formation and finalization of the new covenant. Jesus comes to earth as a child and defeats the devil through His life, death, and resurrection. Because of this, the devil begins to fight against the early Church, causing the great persecution they faced in the years leading up to AD 70. This is the great centerpiece and turning point of Revelation. Everything in the first half of the book leads toward it, and everything in the second half leads from it and is informed by it.[16]

REPETITION IN REVELATION

Revelation is not only filled with symbols that require interpretation, but it is also filled with repetition. The seals, the trumpets, the seven figures, and the bowls all depict the same events of the AD 70 destruction in different ways and from different

[15] Some say the woman is Mary, the mother of Jesus, because she literally birthed Jesus; however, this is a prophetic picture of the group or movement that birthed the Messiah into the world. That group is the faithful remnant of Old Testament Israel.

[16] If Futurists and Historicists understood chiastic arch structure, they would be forced to abandon their systems of interpretation. Both of these systems are predicated upon the idea that Revelation is written in sequential order, but this is not so. Even the fact that Revelation 12 returns to before the birth of Christ clearly throws the idea of the book being sequential to the wayside.

angles. They are not exact parallels, but each repeating picture emphasizes something new. Some might wonder, *Why would the artist paint the picture with repeating patterns? What does this represent?* David Chilton gives a great explanation of why we find four pictures of seven judgments. He writes:

> St. John's prophecy is related to the message of Leviticus 26. Like Deuteronomy 28, Leviticus 26 sets forth the sanctions of the [Mosaic] Covenant: If Israel obeys God, she will be blessed in every area of life (Lev. 26:1–13; Deut. 28:1–14); if she disobeys, however, she will be visited with the Curse, spelled out in horrifying detail (Lev. 26:14–39; Deut. 28:15–68). (These curses were most fully poured out in the progressive desolation of Israel during the Last Days, culminating in the Great Tribulation of A.D. 67–70, as punishment for her apostasy and rejection of her True Husband, the Lord Jesus Christ.) One of the striking features of the Leviticus passage is that the curses are arranged in a special pattern: Four times in this chapter God says, "I will punish you seven times for your sins." (Lev. 26:18, 21, 24, 28). The number *seven,* as we will see abundantly throughout Revelation, is a Biblical number for completeness or fullness (taken from the seven-day pattern laid down at the creation in Genesis 1). [The number seven alone is used fifty-four times in Revelation.] The number *four* is used in Scripture in connection with the earth, especially the Land of Israel; thus four rivers flowed out of Eden to water the whole earth (Gen. 2:10); the Land, like the Altar, is pictured as having four corners (Isa. 11:12; cf. Ex. 27:1-2), from which the four winds blow (Jer. 49:36); the camp of Israel was arranged in four groups around the sides of the Tabernacle (Num. 2); and so on (see your concordance and Bi-

ble Dictionary). So by speaking of four seven-fold judgments in Leviticus 26, God is saying that a full, complete judgment will come upon the Land of Israel for its sins. This theme is taken up by the prophets in their warnings to Israel:

"I will send ***four kinds of destroyers*** *against them," declares the Lord, "the sword to kill and the dogs to drag away and the birds and the wild animals to devour and destroy."* (Jer. 15:3)

"For this is what the Sovereign Lord says: How much worse will it be when I send against Jerusalem my ***four dreadful judgments****—sword and famine and wild beasts and plague—to kill its men and their animals!"* (Ez. 14:21)

The imagery of a sevenfold judgment coming four times is most fully developed in the Book of Revelation, which is explicitly divided into four sets of seven. In thus following the formal structure of the covenantal curse in Leviticus, St. John underscores the nature of his prophecy as a declaration of covenant wrath against Jerusalem.[17]

Building on the fourfold judgment concept that Chilton brings to the surface, I would call us to remember the chiastic arch structure as well.

C – Seven Seals

  D – Seven Trumpets, Angel, Two Witnesses

    E – Woman, Dragon, Male Child

  D – Two Beasts, Angel, Seven Bowls

C – Destruction of Babylon

[17] David Chilton, *Days of Vengance* (Dallas, GA: Dominion Press, 1987), 16–17.

The C's and the D's are very similar to each other. Also, as we have seen with the first C (the Seven Seals), John incorporated many parallels to Matthew 24 and the Olivet Discourse. Revelation is actually quite repetitive, and intentionally so.

Understanding this makes all the difference in the world. Suddenly we are able to see the seals, trumpets, figures, and bowls as different expressions of the same event, not as different and successive events. Though it might seem strange that John did it this way, it actually makes understanding the book much simpler. The big picture gives us a framework for deciphering the smaller elements.

THE BEFORE AND AFTER

The turning point of the events of the book can be further demonstrated by looking at the *before* and the *after* of AD 70. The Lamb's opening of the scroll in Revelation 5 is the beginning of the judgment events that destroy the old covenant and fully establish the new covenant. These events begin with the opening of the seals on the scroll (the first C) and culminate with the destruction of Jerusalem (figuratively Babylon[18]) (the second C). In the middle, in Revelation 12, is the cosmic summary of the spiritual significance of the AD 70 events—the end of the old covenant and the full installation of the new. Thus, we could say that all of Revelation hinges on the *before* and *after* of AD 70. That one event, which is the focus of Revelation, was a turning point in the history of the Church. It is second only to the death, resurrection, and ascension of Christ.

[18] If a historicist can see that Revelation 4–11 is about Jerusalem, as many Historicists do admit, then they cannot escape the outcome of the chiastic prose, which determines that the second half of the arch is in direct relation to the first half of the arch.

Recognizing this brings important clarity to our reading of the Book of Revelation. In the introduction, Jesus tells John, *"Write, therefore, what you have seen, what is now and what will take place later"* (Rev. 1:19). In this verse we see the progression of *before, now,* and *after*. Understanding this is crucial to understanding the book as a whole. The *before* (*"what you have seen"*) is the vision of Jesus on the beach at Patmos and the self-description He spoke to John (Revelation 1). The *now* (*"what is now"*) is John's present-tense communication to the seven churches (Revelation 2–3). He writes to them in the present tense because this is his and their current reality (pre-AD 70). The remainder of Revelation is a prophecy regarding the *after* (*"what will take place later"*) (Revelation 4–22).

In Revelation 4, John is taken to Heaven in a vision, where he witnesses a cosmic worship service involving the twenty-four elders and four living creatures. Then, in chapter 5, he sees a scroll *"with writing on both sides and sealed with seven seals"* (Rev. 5:1). When John discovers that no one in Heaven or earth is worthy to break the seals and open the scroll, he weeps. However, one of the elders tells him, *"Do not weep! See, the Lion of the tribe of Judah, the Root of David, has triumphed. He is able to open the scroll and its seven seals"* (Rev. 5:5). This Lamb, Jesus Christ, takes the scroll. This is the seminal moment when the judgments of God against the old covenant are about to be released, and all of Heaven sings a new song in worship of the Lamb.

Kenneth Gentry, one of the greatest living scholars on this topic, points out that the scroll, which has writing on the inside and outside and is sealed with seven seals, looked like a first-century divorce certificate.[19] John and the early believers would have recognized it as such. In other words, the scroll was

[19] Gentry, *Navigating the Book of Revelation* (Fountain Inn, SC: GoodBirth Ministries, 2011), 45–71.

God's divorce certificate to the great whore of Babylon (Israel of the old covenant). This picture of a divine divorce between God and Israel is mentioned several times in the Old Testament, when Israel walked away from God (see Isa. 50:1; Jer. 3:8). Here, God makes that divorce final. In this, God was not divorcing Himself from a group of people but from the old covenant. He then steps into the new covenant with both Jews and gentiles.

What we must understand, as we read this, is that when John is taken up to Heaven in Revelation 4, he sees God the Father, but Jesus is not mentioned. John is experiencing prophetically what it was like *before* Jesus arrived back in Heaven as the victor. Then, in Revelation 5:1–4, we find this scene:

> *Then I saw in the right hand of him who sat on the throne a scroll with writing on both sides and sealed with seven seals. And I saw a mighty angel proclaiming in a loud voice, "Who is worthy to break the seals and open the scroll?" But no one in heaven or on earth or under the earth could open the scroll or even look inside it. I wept and wept because no one was found who was worthy to open the scroll or look inside.*

When John weeps at the unopened scroll, it is a heart-rending moment—a picture of Heaven without a victorious Jesus. It is difficult to even comprehend such a place. This is the *before*. Thankfully, John continues:

> *Then one of the elders said to me, "Do not weep! See, the Lion of the tribe of Judah, the Root of David, has triumphed. He is able to open the scroll and its seven seals." Then I saw a Lamb, looking as if it had been slain, standing at the center of the throne, encircled by the four living creatures and the elders. The Lamb had seven horns and seven eyes, which are the seven spirits of God sent out into all the earth* (Revelation 5:5–6).

Now, John experiences what it is like to see Jesus unveiled as the victor who can open the scroll, end the old covenant, and forever establish the new covenant. This is the *after.* Revelation 4 is part of John's prophetic vision, but it first shows what *was* before showing *what is to come.*[20] When Jesus the slain Lamb takes the scroll and begins to open the seals, He is systematically removing the old covenant and establishing the new. This is what the first-century Church was looking forward to—the end of the old covenant temple system. This event changed history and our reality as Christians in ways many of us have not understood.

For example, if we do not understand the significance of the *before* and *after,* we will see the worship service of Revelation 4 as our current reality. We will think we should imitate the twenty-four elders and throw our crowns down at God's feet. However, the elders were doing this in the picture of what it was like *before* Jesus was revealed as the Lamb who was slain. Their reality before Jesus arrived on the scene is not our current reality. We know this is true because, in His letters to the seven churches, Jesus promises to give victor's crowns to His faithful followers, and He tells them not to let anyone take their crowns from them (see Rev. 2:10; 3:11). Jesus also promises authority and rulership to His followers (see Rev. 2:26–27; 3:21). These promises would be fulfilled through His coming in judgment in AD 70, as spelled out in the remainder of Revelation.

This means these promises to the faithful believers in Revelation are not future for us; they are available to us right now, because we live on the other side of AD 70. Unlike the twenty-four elders, we are not required to cast our crowns at the

[20] This is dramatically different from those that teach that Revelation 4:1 is referencing a future rapture of the Church. That theory isn't possible considering that, according to John's vision, Jesus doesn't even arrive back in Heaven as the Lamb slain until Revelation 5!

feet of Jesus. Instead, He invites us to sit on His throne and to rule the nations with Him. When He took the scroll and opened its seals, ending the old covenant, He made us *"a kingdom and priests to serve our God,"* those who *"will reign on the earth"* (Rev. 5:10). This is our identity in God's new covenant Kingdom. He does not give us crowns so that we can throw them down. He gives us crowns so that we can rule alongside Him as His Bride.

The events of AD 70 changed things. It was the culmination of the events that began with Jesus' death, resurrection, and ascension. It was the final page in the chapter of the old covenant. This is the central theme of the Book of Revelation, the middle point in the chiastic arch. Understanding this structure brings incredible clarity to what the details of the Book of Revelation are actually about.

PART TWO

THE NINE MAJOR COMPONENTS

Now that we have looked at the big picture context of the painting—the *when, how, why,* and *where*—we are going to take a few steps closer in order to examine its major elements. No longer are we looking at the bigger picture, but neither are we looking at the minute details. The Book of Revelation is comprised of nine main elements—an introduction, seven visions, and an epilogue. Each of these visions is added on top of the previous vision so that the "painting" has a layering effect.

Here's the breakdown:

- The Introduction (Rev. 1:1–7)
- First Vision—The Seven Churches (Rev. 1:8–3:22)
- Second Vision—The Seven Seals (Rev. 4:1–8:5)
- Third Vision—The Seven Trumpets (Rev. 8:6–11:19)
- Fourth Vision—Followers of the Lamb or the Beast (Rev. 12–14)
- Fifth Vision—The Seven Bowls of Wrath (Rev. 15-16)
- Sixth Vision—The Babylonian Harlot (Rev. 17–19:21)
- Seventh Vision—The New Heavens and New Earth (Rev. 20:1–22:11)
- The Epilogue (Rev 22:12–21)

These nine components are the main focus of the remainder of this book. Although we will not examine in detail most of the specific imagery used in Revelation, studying these nine major components will provide us with important interpretive keys. They give us a lens through which we can effectively study the book in more depth. Though this short book is merely an introduction to the complex and beautiful painting of Revelation, my hope is that it provides a necessary foundation for more in-depth study.

THE INTRODUCTION (REVELATION 1)

Revelation begins with John's announcement of its name, The Revelation of Jesus Christ, and his promise that the events prophesied within it will happen very soon. Then, he shares his first dramatic vision, in which the risen Christ appears to him. This vision is separate from the out-of-body experiences that John records in Revelation 4–22. Here in chapter 1, John is in his Patmos context when Jesus walks up from behind. John records it like this:

> *I turned around to see the voice that was speaking to me. And when I turned I saw seven golden lampstands, and among the lampstands was someone like a son of man, dressed in a robe reaching down to his feet and with a golden sash around his chest. The hair on his head was white like wool, as white as snow, and his eyes were like blazing fire. His feet were like bronze glowing in a furnace, and his voice was like the sound of rushing waters. In his right hand he held seven stars, and coming out of his mouth was a sharp, double-edged sword. His face was like the sun shining in all its brilliance. When I saw him, I fell at his feet as though dead. Then he placed his right hand on me and said: "Do not be afraid. I am the First and the Last. I am the Living One; I was dead, and now look, I am*

> *alive forever and ever! And I hold the keys of death and Hades"* (Revelation 1:12–18).

This encounter is crucial to understanding the seven letters that follow in Revelation 2–3. After Jesus appears to John in this way, He commands John to write to the seven churches. Each of these letters is dictated to John by Jesus, so they are written in the first person from Jesus to the members of these churches. In them, Jesus not only addresses the specific situation of each church, but He also disperses the visionary revelation of Himself that He has just shown to John. These self-descriptions, which appear at the beginning of each letter, are each a small selection from the larger description given in Revelation 1:12–18. Here is the way Jesus chose to reveal Himself to each church:

1. Ephesus—He holds the seven stars and walks among the seven lampstands (see Rev. 2:1).
2. Smyrna—He is the First and Last, the Living One (see Rev. 2:8).
3. Pergamum—He has the sharp, double-edged sword in His mouth (see Rev. 2:12, 16).
4. Thyatira—He is the Son of God, whose eyes are like fire and His feet like bronze (see Rev. 2:18).
5. Sardis—He holds the seven spirits of God and the seven stars (see Rev. 3:1).
6. Philadelphia—He is holy and true, and He holds the key of David (see Rev. 3:7).
7. Laodicea—He is the faithful and true witness, the ruler of God's creation (see Rev. 3:14).

Here we see that John (in obedience to Jesus' direction) takes the revelation of Jesus he has just received, and he disperses it in the seven letters. The big picture revelation of the risen Jesus is spread out among the seven churches in Revelation 2–3. This is a beautiful picture of how His body knows in part (see 1 Cor. 13:9). The Spirit takes the big picture revelation of Scripture that God has given to all of us, and He applies it individually and contextually to us in a way that we will each understand and that will be uniquely meaningful. We all see part of who Jesus is, but none of us sees Him fully or perfectly yet. Thus, we need to work together and learn from each other to begin to see the whole picture of Christ. This is why every joint in the body of Christ must supply its part or its unique perspective (see Eph. 4:16).

Further, Jesus purposefully presents Himself to each of the churches in a way that was historically and culturally relevant to them. These statements were not just general facts about the nature of Christ; they were specific pieces of revelation intended to deeply connect with the hearts and situations of these churches. For example, to Pergamum, the seat of the Roman capital in Asia Minor, Jesus reveals Himself as the one with a sword, the true authority in the earth. In Thyatira, a metal tradesman city, Jesus reveals Himself as the one with eyes like fire and feet of burnished bronze. Jesus knows exactly which revelation will be the most personal and meaningful to His readers.

In the seven letters, Jesus delivers His prophecies in a very personal manner. He gives each church a piece of revelation regarding what He is like and who He is that is especially applicable to them in their situation. This is a picture of how the gift of prophecy is used within the body of Christ.

Anyone who has prophesied to others can testify that God will use specific words, ideas, and images to get a message to a person in a way that will uniquely and powerfully touch that person's heart. If any other person had received that particular word or image, it probably would not have been nearly as impactful. Often, that word may seem strange to the person delivering it, but the one who receives it knows exactly what it means. This is because God knows exactly what will most speak to each person's heart. He knows each one of us intimately, and He knows how to say, "I love you," to a thousand different people in a thousand different ways. Here, Jesus practically demonstrates for us how personal prophecy is applied and delivered. In His use of prophecy, we see not only God's heart and loving care for us as individuals, but also the beautiful and masterful layering and structure of these letters. Further, by starting this book with this sort of personal prophecy, Jesus sets the tone for the rest of the prophecy as something that is written in the language and symbolism uniquely applicable and meaningful to the people it was being written for in the first century.

After Jesus' great revelation of Himself to John, He makes an important statement that helps us understand the structure of the revelation of Christ more completely: *"Write, therefore, what you have seen, what is now and what will take place later"* (Rev. 1:19). This verse divides the content of Revelation into three parts, past, present, and future. The vision of Jesus in Revelation 1:1–18 that John had just seen was *"what you have seen."* That was the past. The letters to the seven churches in Revelation 2–3 was *"what is now."* This was the reality that existed in John's present. The material that John would see in the heavenlies, in Revelation 4–22, was *"what will take place later."* This transition from present to future is made clear by the invitation in Revelation 4:1, *"Come up here, and I will show you what must take place after this."* John only begins to see the future after he is pulled up into the heavenlies.

As mentioned previously, viewing these timeframes through a historical and contextual grid, we can see that the "what was" and the "what is" of Revelation 1–3 lead up to the "what will be" of the remainder of the book. These are the events of AD 70—the destruction of Jerusalem and the old covenant system. This was obvious to John's first-century readers; however, it has escaped many modern-day readers. The reason is simple. Revelation is deeply symbolic, and it uses symbols that would have been meaningful in the first-century Jewish context. But these once-clear symbols are mysterious to us because we live in a different era and culture.

The first step to decoding the symbolism of Revelation is acknowledging that it is symbolic. Some people argue that they take Revelation literally, but the reality is, it is impossible to take the book completely literally, because the entire planet would be destroyed by chapter 6, when the sun turns black and all the stars in the sky fall upon the earth. If such an event literally occurred, there would be no need for the remaining chapters of Revelation. Instead, we must acknowledge that the book is full of symbolism. We see this from the start, even in Jesus' description of Himself in chapter 1. He says:

> *The mystery of the seven stars that you saw in my right hand and of the seven golden lampstands is this: The seven stars are the angels of the seven churches, and the seven lampstands are the seven churches* (Revelation 1:20).

Here Jesus plainly tells John that the stars and lampstands are symbolic. They are a mystery that must be interpreted, and He gives the interpretation. The seven lampstands symbolize the seven churches, and the seven stars in His right hand symbolize the angels of those churches. This might seem like a strange arrangement—having an apostle write and deliver letters to spirit beings known as angels—until we realize that stars are used symbolically throughout the Bible to speak of local government, and the Greek word *angelos,* which is translated here as "angels," simply means "messenger or envoy."[21] Knowing this, we can gather that the seven stars/angels refer to the local leadership of the seven churches.

Thus we see, in the introduction, two important themes that carry through the rest of the book. First, it is a deeply personal and historically contextual prophecy written to specific people in specific circumstances. And second, because of this, the book is deeply symbolic, using imagery that was common in the first century but that appears mysterious to us in the twenty-first century.

[21] For example, Joseph's dream in Genesis 37:5–11 was instantly recognized as foretelling his ascendancy to a ruling position, not the literal sun, moon, and stars bowing down to him.

VISION 1: THE SEVEN CHURCHES (REVELATION 2–3)

In chapter 4, we looked at the structure of the Book of Revelation, which is written as a chiastic arch. It forms an arch of meaning that looks like this:

A

B

C

D

C

B

A

In this arch, the first A and the second A mirror each other, yet they are slightly different too, because the second A comes after and is impacted by the main event at D. This is important for us to understand. It helps us know how to view the events and people of the first ABC, who precede the main event of D, which is the destruction of Jerusalem in AD 70. The spiritual situation of the Christians who lived before AD 70 was not identical to ours. We live on the other side of the chiastic arch, and the spiritual realities of the Kingdom were forever changed by the crucial events of AD 70. However, we can learn important lessons from the lives of the early believers and Jesus' letters to the seven churches of Revelation.

Like the entire Book of Revelation, the seven letters to the churches are organized as a smaller chiastic arch.

A – Ephesus

B – Smyrna

C – Pergamum

D – Thyatira

C – Sardis

B – Philadelphia

A – Laodicea

In accord with this poetic form, the central letter to Thyatira is the longest and most important letter. In it, the main message is against compromise. To those who do not compromise, Jesus promises:

> *I will give authority over the nations— that one "will rule them with an iron scepter and will dash them to pieces like pottery"—just as I have received authority from my Father* (Revelation 2:26–27).

This promise echoes the messianic description of Jesus in Psalm 2 and Revelation 12 (which, like Thyatira, is also the centerpiece of a chiasm). Just as Jesus is the one who *"will rule all the nations with an iron scepter"* (Rev. 12:5), so too, His faithful followers will rule over the nations, alongside Christ, with an iron scepter. *Our co-reigning is a key theme of both chiastic arches*—both the big arch of Revelation and the smaller arch of the seven letters.

The first three and last three letters, which lead up to and away from the centerpiece, also parallel each other in certain ways. For example, Ephesus and Laodicea, the first and last churches (A), both receive a rebuke for complacency and the threat of losing their church. Jesus threatens to remove Ephesus' lampstand, and He threatens to spit Laodicea from His mouth.

Likewise, both of the B churches (Smyrna and Philadelphia) are in the midst of intense persecution and receive a positive commendation from Jesus.

The C churches also receive rebukes, but specifically phrased in terms of attack. Jesus warns Pergamum that He will fight against them with the sword of His mouth if they do not repent. And to Sardis, He issues the threat of a midnight attack, like a thief in the night.

Beyond this parallelism, the chiastic arch structure points to two ideas that bring greater depth to these letters: a picture of history and the victor sayings.

A PICTURE OF HISTORY

The first idea is that the seven letters actually imitate biblical history.[22] Seeing these letters in the light of biblical history adds richness to their new covenant meaning. Here is how the chiasm mirrors biblical history:

A – Ephesus (the Garden)

B – Smyrna (the Exodus)

C – Pergamum (the Wilderness)

D – Thyatira (the Monarchy)

[22] Chilton, *The Days of Vengeance* (Dallas, GA: Dominion Press, 1987), 86–89.

C – Sardis (the Exile)

B – Philadelphia (the Rebuilding)

A – Laodicea (the Casting Out)

In Ephesus, Jesus promises, *"To the one who is victorious, I will give the right to eat from the tree of life, which is in the paradise of God"* (Rev. 2:7). This is a picture of the Garden of Eden, where the tree of life stood. In Smyrna, Jesus tells them they will face a ten-day tribulation, followed by victory (see Rev. 2:10). This mirrors the ten plagues, which were followed by the victory of Israel and their exodus from Egypt. Then, in Pergamum, Jesus mentions Balaam and Balak, who enticed the Israelites into sin during their journey through the wilderness (see Rev. 2:14).

In Thyatira, the centerpiece, the believers are promised authority to rule and a rod of iron. These refer back to King David and the monarchy. The monarchy was the turning point for Israel. It took them from continually building and journeying to a place of identity and stability. It was the Golden Age of Israel, especially under David and Solomon's rule. Thus, Thyatira, the turning point of the arch aligns with the turning point of biblical history. It was the climax of history, and from there on out, Israel digressed.

In Sardis, Jesus addresses those who have a reputation for being alive but are actually spiritually dead. He tells them to repent and awake (see Rev. 3:1–2). This mirrors the period of the exile to Babylon and Assyria in the Old Testament, when only a remnant of the Jews remained faithful to God. Then in Philadelphia, we find the theme of rebuilding, which parallels the next season in biblical history—the rebuilding of Jerusalem under Nehemiah and Ezra. The faithful in Philadelphia are promised a new Jerusalem, just like those who returned from exile were able to rebuild their city.

Lastly, Laodicea is a picture of what is coming for Israel in the first century, when in AD 70 they are literally cast out, or spit out of God's mouth, through the destruction of Jerusalem and the Temple. In His letter to Laodicea, Jesus threatens to spit them out of His mouth if they do not return to Him; this echoes the threat of Leviticus, where God promises the Israelites that if they break their covenant with Him He will vomit them out of the land (see Lev. 18:25, 28; 20:22). The letter to Laodicea, then, in a sense prophesies what is about to happen to the old covenant Israel. In this way, the chiastic arch returns full circle to the Garden, where Adam and Eve were cast out for rebelling against God.

In these seven letters, then, we get a picture of the progression of the people of God from the Garden of Eden to the high point of the monarchy under David until they are eventually once again cast out of the land. In this way, this structure demonstrates the completeness of biblical history, from the Garden of Eden to AD 70. It has come to an end, just as it started, and now it is time for something altogether new—the new covenant.

THE VICTOR SAYINGS

A second idea imbedded in the seven letters has to do with the seven victor sayings or promises. In the chiastic arch that forms the Book of Revelation, the seven letters are the first B, and the Bride of Christ is the second B on the other side of the arch.

A – Greeting

B – Seven Churches

C – Seven Seals

D – Seven Trumpets, Angel, Two Witnesses

E – Woman, Dragon, Male Child

D – Two Beasts, Angel, Seven Bowls

C – Destruction of Babylon

B – Bride

A – Epilogue

Thus, the Church transitions from its earlier state on the first half of the arch, pre-AD 70, to the fullness of its position as the Bride of Christ on the second half of the arch. We see this in the outworking of these victor sayings. Each of the promises Jesus makes in the seven letters is fulfilled in the Bride of Christ near the end of Revelation.

In the first letter, to Ephesus, Jesus promises *"the right to eat from the tree of life"* (Rev. 2:7). The parallel from the end of Revelation says that the righteous *"have the right to the tree of life"* (Rev. 22:14). So, on one side of the arch is the promise of the right to eat from the tree of life, and on the other side of the arch is the fulfillment of that promise.

This is significant and meaningful for us today, because it shows the progression that happened from *before* AD 70 to *after* AD 70. Before, the believers were promised certain things; after AD 70, the believers received the experience of these promises as the Bride of Christ. After the complete and final victory of AD 70, all believers are now able to eat from the tree of life. We are not waiting for this promise or any of the other promises of these letters to be fulfilled. This pattern is repeated in the remaining six letters. As mentioned previously, though the promises are addressed to specific churches, they are meant for all the faithful believers of the first century. Now, in the years since AD 70, their fulfillment applies to all believers.

To Smyrna, Jesus promises resurrection. They do not need to fear the second death (see Rev. 2:10–11). On the other side of the arch, Revelation 20:6 tells us about the fulfillment of this promise in the first resurrection:

> *Blessed and holy are those who share in the first resurrection. The second death has no power over them, but they will be priests of God and of Christ and will reign with him for a thousand years.*

Jesus promises to the believers at Pergamum that He will give them the hidden manna and white stones *"with a new name written on it, known only to the one who receives it"* (Rev. 2:17). By the end of Revelation, Christ's name is written on their foreheads (see Rev. 22:4), and they are invited to the wedding supper of the Lamb (see Rev. 19:9). They are brought into this private feast, which the white stones gave them access to.[23]

In Thyatira, Jesus promises authority over the nations (see Rev. 2:26–27). Then, in Revelation 20:4, there are *"thrones on which were seated those who had been given authority to judge."* Because of their faithfulness to Christ, they are given the authority to rule with Christ and judge the nations. Jesus also promises the believers at Thyatira the morning star (see Rev. 2:28). At the other end of the arch, Jesus reveals Himself as *"the bright Morning Star"* (Rev. 22:16). He is the fulfillment of the promise, which is a promise of Himself and the authority to rule with Him.

To Sardis, Jesus promises to give them clean, white clothing and guarantees that their names will never be blotted from the Book of Life (see Rev. 3:4–5). At the end of Revelation, we find those who have washed robes (see Rev. 22:14) and *"those whose names are written in the Lamb's book of life"* (Rev. 21:27).

---

[23] In the first century, white stones were used to grant access to great public festivals. For more see my book, "*Understanding the Seven Churches of Revelation*" pages 84–86.

To the church at Philadelphia, Jesus promises to make them pillars in the Temple of God and to write on them the names of God, the new Jerusalem (*"which is coming down out of heaven from my God"*), and Christ (see Rev. 3:12). Near the end of Revelation, God's name is written on His followers (see Rev. 22:4). We see the new Jerusalem, which is the Bride of Christ, descending out of Heaven (see Rev. 21:2, 10), and *"the Lord God Almighty and the Lamb are its temple"* (Rev. 21:22). If God and Christ are the Temple of the new covenant, believers are the pillars in the Temple. They are hidden with Christ in God, as Colossians 3:3 says. This is the divine union of the new covenant.

In the old covenant Temple, people came to meet with God, but they could not dwell in Him. The new covenant gives us a different picture. The new Jerusalem is the Bride (the believers in Christ), and in it, the Temple is God, and within the Temple are pillars, which are the believers. These overlapping pictures of Christ in us and us in Him show the incredible union that new covenant believers are welcomed into.

Finally, in Laodicea the believers are promised *"the right to sit with me on my throne"* (Rev. 3:21). This is fulfilled in Revelation 20:4, where the martyrs are given thrones to sit on and rule the nations with Christ. In this way, each of the promises from the seven letters finds fulfillment before the end of Revelation.

As mentioned earlier, a picture of the entire story of the new covenant transition is laid out in the central chapter of Revelation 12, which is the center of the chiasm. It leads from the promises *before* to the fulfillment of the promises *after*. As the early Church looked ahead to the coming destruction, the Book of Revelation (which was originally a letter to them) reassured them of the promises and their soon coming fulfillment on the other side of the Great Tribulation, when Israel would be vomited from the land. As they faced a terrible and traumatic time,

Jesus used these letters to reassure the early believers of their safety in God's heart and of victory on the other side. For us, looking back at that time in history, we can be confident that what the early Church looked forward to is now ours in fullness. We are not struggling to be victorious; we start from the place of victory. Because of what is behind us, historically and spiritually, we have inherited all of Christ's promises by faith. This is one of the most important modern applications that we can glean from the seven letters of Revelation.

VISION 2: THE SEVEN SEALS (REVELATION 4:1–8:5)

Now, having covered the introduction and the letters to the seven churches, we will examine some of the more challenging parts of Revelation.

After Jesus appears to John on Patmos and dictates the seven letters to him, John then enters an out-of-body experience in which he is carried to the throne room in Heaven. There, as recorded in Revelation 4 and 5, John sees God the Father on His throne. This is similar to the visions of Isaiah 6 and Ezekiel 1. As John watches, a scroll of judgment is brought forth that cannot be opened until Jesus, as the slain Lamb, appears and begins to open the scroll of judgment. This shows that judgment was not to be poured out until after the new covenant had been established by Jesus' death on the cross and His ascension into Heaven. Therefore, we can know that Revelation 4 and 5 are not describing something in our future. Instead, the narrative of these chapters actually starts at a point before Jesus' crucifixion. Then He appears in Heaven as the slain Lamb who is able to open the scrolls. All this happened in the first century.

Many scholars agree that the chapters that follow, Revelation 6–8, are a parallel of Matthew 24,[24] although they debate

[24] For example, see the sections on Revelation 6:1–8 in *Come Lord Jesus* by the Futurist Watchman Nee.

the timing of Matthew 24's fulfillment.[25] Let's briefly look at the major components of these chapters and how they parallel Matthew 24.

SEAL 1: HORSEMAN 1

The first seal and horseman symbolize conquest, a parallel to *"nation rising against nation"* in Matthew 24:7. This refers to the fragmenting of the Pax Romana (Roman Peace) of the first century. This was the only time in history when world peace was achieved, although it was achieved through oppression and conquering. The dissolution of peace served as a sign of the coming of the events Jesus had prophesied.

SEAL 2: HORSEMAN 2

The first seal and horseman clearly lead to the second seal and horseman, which symbolize the *"wars and rumors of war"* in Matthew 24:6.

SEAL 3: HORSEMAN 3

The third seal and horseman clearly symbolize famine, mirroring Matthew 24:7's prophecy of the widespread first-century famines. Interestingly, in this picture, John hears this detail:

> *Then I heard what sounded like a voice among the four living creatures, saying, "Two pounds of wheat for a day's wages, and six pounds of barley for a day's wages, and do not damage the oil and the wine"* (Revelation 6:6).

[25] In my book, *Raptureless*, I specifically address how every detail of Matthew 24 came to pass in AD 70.

According to Robert Mounce, this means the price had risen 1,000 percent from its former price. The first-century Jewish historian Josephus recorded much regarding the unbelievable famine that occurred in AD 67–70.[26] From his records, we know this famine lived up to these awful predictions.

SEAL 4: HORSEMAN 4

The fourth seal and horseman symbolize the sword, plagues, famine, and death—the natural outcomes caused by the first three horsemen of conquest, war, and famine.

SEAL 5: MARTYRS

The fifth seal gives a picture of martyrs crying out to God for judgment. These are the Christians who were persecuted and martyred during AD 30–70. In this vision, they cry out to God, "How much longer?" The implication in the first century was "How much longer until the AD 70 destruction occurs?" They were calling for God's judgment against the old covenant and the apostate nation of Israel, not for Jesus' final return. Jesus spoke of this in the story of the widow:

> *Then Jesus told his disciples a parable to show them that they should always pray and not give up. He said: "In a certain town there was a judge who neither feared God nor cared what people thought. And there was a widow in that town who kept coming to him with the plea, 'Grant me justice against my adversary.' "For some time he refused. But finally he said to himself, 'Even though I don't fear God or care what people*

[26] Robert Mounce, *The Book of Revelation* (Grand Rapids, MI: William B. Eerdmans, 1977), 155.

> *think, yet because this widow keeps bothering me, I will see that she gets justice, so that she won't eventually come and attack me!'" And the Lord said,* ***"Listen to what the unjust judge says. And will not God bring about justice for his chosen ones, who cry out to him day and night? Will he keep putting them off? I tell you, he will see that they get justice, and quickly.*** *However, when the Son of Man comes, will he find faith on the earth?"* (Luke 18:1–8).

In context, this clearly speaks of the first-century believers (including those who had been martyred) crying out to God and petitioning Him to bring His justice on their behalf. In other words, they were praying for the release of the AD 70 judgment against Jerusalem, which would stop the Jewish persecution of Christians.

SEAL 6: AN EARTHQUAKE, THE HEAVENS SHAKEN, THE 144,000 SEALED, AND THE GREAT MULTITUDE IN WHITE ROBES

If we are to read the Book of Revelation literally, as some suggest, then the book would end at Revelation 6:12–14:

> *I watched as he opened the sixth seal. There was a great earthquake. The sun turned black like sackcloth made of goat hair, the whole moon turned blood red, and the stars in the sky fell to earth, as figs drop from a fig tree when shaken by a strong wind. The heavens receded like a scroll being rolled up, and every mountain and island was removed from its place.*

If these words are to be read as literal events, and not as prophetic language that needs interpretation, then we don't need the rest of the Book of Revelation, because these three verses alone would be enough to end human life on this planet.

Instead, I believe the most sensible understanding is that the sixth seal contains several events that together symbolize the destruction of Jerusalem in AD 70.

The first event of the sixth seal is an earthquake that shakes the heavens and the earth. This parallels Matthew 24:29:

> *Immediately after the distress of those days "the sun will be darkened, and the moon will not give its light; the stars will fall from the sky, and the heavenly bodies will be shaken."*

The margin notes for Matthew 24:29 in most English translations suggest that Jesus was using the Jewish prophetic lingo of His day and referring back to Isaiah 13:10 and 34:4. Saying that the heavenly bodies would be disturbed was a way of saying that a city or government was going to be judged.

In the wake of this judgment, John sees how the people of the land will respond:

> *Then the kings of the earth, the princes, the generals, the rich, the mighty, and everyone else, both slave and free, hid in caves and among the rocks of the mountains. They called to the mountains and the rocks,* ***"Fall on us and hide us from the face of him who sits on the throne and from the wrath of the Lamb! For the great day of their wrath has come, and who can withstand it?"*** (Revelation 6:15–17).

This is eerily similar to the warning Jesus gave as He was being taken to the cross:

> *Jesus turned and said to them, "Daughters of Jerusalem, do not weep for me;* ***weep for yourselves and for your children.*** *For the time will come when you will say, 'Blessed are the childless women, the wombs that never bore and the breasts that never nursed!' Then "'they will say to the mountains,*

> ***"Fall on us!" and to the hills, "Cover us!"' For if people do these things when the tree is green, what will happen when it is dry?"*** (Luke 23:28–31).

Both passages indicate the great mourning and terror that the people who lived through the destruction of Jerusalem would experience. In the same way that John used Matthew 24 as a dramatic parallel of the seven seals, so also he referenced this passage in Luke 23.

The second event of the sixth seal is the sealing of the 144,000. This number is 12 x 12 x 1000, and it symbolizes wholeness. It represents the entire first-century Christian community, which followed Jesus' instructions in Matthew 24:15–21 and fled to the nearby mountains of Pella. As a result, not one Christian died in the destruction of AD 70.[27] This also parallels Ezekiel 9:4 and the sealing of the faithful.

> *And said to him, "Go throughout the city of Jerusalem and put a mark on the foreheads of those who grieve and lament over all the detestable things that are done in it"* (Ezekiel 9:4).

The Book of Revelation contains two marks, a mark of the Lamb (here in Rev 7:3) and a mark of the Beast (in Rev. 13:16–17).

The third event of the sixth seal gives us another glimpse of the martyred saints, this time post-judgment. Since the sixth seal pictures the destruction of Jerusalem, with the shaking of the heavens and earth and the 144,000 (the entire Christian community) fleeing to Mount Pella for protection, we know this group in white robes is the same as the group in the fifth seal. Now they are pictured after their pleas for justice have

[27] Eusebius, *The Church History*, Vol 3, chapter 5, section 3.

been fulfilled in the AD 70 destruction.

SEAL 7: SILENCE FOR THIRTY MINUTES

Though the need for thirty minutes of silence seems obscure to us, to the Jews of the first century, what was happening during those thirty minutes would have been obvious. We find a clue about this in Alfred Edersheim's description of the offering of incense in the Temple.

> Slowly the incensing priest and his assistants ascended the steps to the Holy Place, preceded by the two priests who had formerly dressed the altar and the candlestick, and who now removed the vessels they had left behind, and, worshipping, withdrew.
>
> Next, one of the assistants reverently spread the coals on the golden altar; the other arranged the incense; and then the chief officiating priest was left alone within the Holy Place, to await the signal of the president before burning the incense. It was probably while thus expectant that the angel Gabriel appeared to Zacharias [Luke 1:8–11].
>
> As the president gave the word of command, which marked that 'the time of incense had come,' 'the whole multitude of the people without' withdrew from the inner court, and fell down before the Lord, spreading their hands in silent prayer.
>
> It is this most solemn period, when throughout the vast Temple buildings deep silence rested on the worshipping multitude, while within the sanctuary itself the

> priest laid the incense on the golden altar, and the cloud of 'odors' [Rev. 5:8] rose up before the Lord, which serves as the image of heavenly things in this description.[28]

This period of silence was a usual part of Temple worship, when the priest put the incense on the altar and all the people silently bowed down before the Lord in awe. The scholar Milton Terry confirms Edersheim's insights, applying them to the seventh seal in Revelation 6:

> Perhaps the idea of this silence was suggested by the cessation of singers and trumpets when King Hezekiah and those with him bowed themselves in reverent worship (2 Chron. 29:28–29), and the half hour may have some reference to the offering of incense described in verses 3 and 4, for that would be about the length of time necessary for a priest to enter the temple and offer incense and return.[29]

Simply put, the reason for thirty minutes of silence in John's writing would have been obvious to any practicing Jew in the first century. This was the time when the priest was offering incense and all the people in the Temple bowed in reverent silence. John is showing the same event take place in the heavenly Temple.

This is the final seal. In the progression of these seals, we see the war and suffering leading up to the destruction of Jerusalem, the protection of the Christians, and finally the incense on the altar and the worship of God in Heaven.

---

[28] Alfred Edersheim, *The Temple: Its Ministry and Services as They Were at the Time of Jesus Christ* (Grand Rapids, MI: William B. Eerdmans, 1980), 167f.

[29] Milton S. Terry, *Biblical Apocalyptics: A Study of the Most Notable Revelations of God and of Christ in the Canonical Scriptures* (New York: Eaton and Mains, 1898), 343f.

VISION 3: THE SEVEN TRUMPETS (REVELATION 8:6–11:19)

Following the seven seals picture of AD 70, John writes about seven trumpets. These also give us a picture of the destruction of Jerusalem. In his use of trumpets, it is possible that John was comparing Jerusalem to the evil Old Testament city of Jericho, which the Israelites conquered by marching around its walls and blowing trumpets. We can see the similarities in God's instructions to Joshua regarding the attack upon Jericho:

> *The Lord said to Joshua, "See, I have given Jericho into your hand, with its king and the valiant warriors. You shall march around the city, all the men of war circling the city once. You shall do so for six days.* ***Also seven priests shall carry seven trumpets of rams' horns before the ark; then on the seventh day you shall march around the city seven times, and the priests shall blow the trumpets****. It shall be that when they make a long blast with the ram's horn, and when you hear the sound of the trumpet, all the people shall shout with a great shout; and the wall of the city will fall down flat, and the people will go up every man straight ahead."* (Joshua 6:2–5 NASB).

Joshua followed God's instructions regarding the seven priests with seven trumpets walking before the ark of the covenant exactly, and the walls fell just as God had said they would. Revelation parallels this passage in Joshua 6 when seven angels (rather than priests) blow seven trumpets and then the ark of the covenant follows them. The only time that the ark of the covenant is mentioned in Revelation is directly following the seventh trumpet.

> *Then God's temple in heaven was opened, and within his temple was seen* ***the ark of his covenant****. And there came flashes of lightning, rumblings, peals of thunder, an earthquake and a severe hailstorm"* (Revelation 11:19).

This placement of the ark of the covenant in the book confirms that John was using the seven trumpets of Jericho's judgment as a parallel to the seven trumpets of Jerusalem's judgment. The ark of the covenant is mentioned at the blast of the seventh trumpet in both stories, indicating the release of the judgment. Let's look now at each trumpet and what it shows us about the judgment events in AD 70.

TRUMPET 1: HAIL AND FIRE RAIN DOWN

After the first trumpet, hail and fire rain down upon the *local land* (*ge*) of Israel. We will examine the hail more specifically when we get to the parallel seventh bowl judgment.

TRUMPET 2: A MOUNTAIN THROWN INTO THE SEA

The symbol of the second trumpet has been distorted by many over the last two thousand years. The most popular recent theory suggests that an asteroid will crash into the ocean and kill a third of the sea creatures and destroy a third of all ships. In reality, if an asteroid that big was going to crash into the earth, it would end the story of the Book of Revelation right there. Such an asteroid would literally move earth off its axis, and all life on earth would immediately either burn up or freeze as the planet moved closer to or away from the sun.

Clearly, this is a symbol. So, we must ask ourselves, *What would the mountain represent to John's readers?* The most obvious answer is that the first century Jewish believers would have interpreted this mountain in Revelation as a symbol of Jerusalem, which was often called God's holy mountain (see Exod. 15:17). David Chilton also gives us a stunning insight on this passage.

> Connect this [Revelation 8:8] with the fact that Jesus, in the middle of a lengthy series of discourses and parables about the destruction of Jerusalem (Matt. 20–25), cursed an unfruitful fig tree, as a symbol of judgment upon Israel. He then told His disciples, "Truly I say to you, if you have faith, and do not doubt, you shall say to this mountain, 'Be taken up and cast into the sea,' it shall happen. And all things you ask in prayer, believing, you shall receive' (Matt. 21:21–22). Was Jesus being flippant? Did He really expect His disciples to go around praying about moving literal mountains? Of course not. More importantly, Jesus was not changing the subject. He was still giving them a lesson about the fall of Israel. What was the lesson? Jesus was instructing His disciples to pray imprecatory prayers, beseeching God to destroy Israel, to wither the fig tree, to cast the apostate mountain into the sea.
>
> And that is exactly what happened. The persecuted Church, under the oppression from the apostate Jews, began praying for God's vengeance upon Israel (Rev. 6:9–11), calling for the mountain of Israel to "be taken up

> and cast into the sea." Their offerings were received at God's heavenly altar, and in response God directed His angels to throw down His judgments to the Land (Rev. 8:3-5).[30]

Thus, in amazing simplicity, the mountain being thrown into the sea is a symbol of Jerusalem's destruction.

Also, it's important to notice the repetition of pictures between the elements of the chiastic arch. In the seven seals, we saw a more general picture of mountains being moved: *"The heavens receded like a scroll being rolled up, and every mountain and island was removed from its place"* (Rev. 6:14). Here in the seven trumpets the picture gets clearer as we move toward the climax of the center of the chiastic arch.

TRUMPET 3: A STAR FALLING

The first-century audience would have easily understood the third trumpet, a falling star named Wormwood that turns a third of the water into wormwood. Modern readers seem to gloss over the mention of wormwood and focus entirely on the falling star. However, knowing the definition of *wormwood* is key to interpreting this passage. *Wormwood* is a specific term used in the Old Testament to warn Israel of its destruction as a punishment for apostasy. We see this clearly in Deuteronomy, where God compares those who turn away from Him to serve other gods to a root that produces wormwood (or bitterness).

> *So that there may not be among you man or woman or family or tribe, whose heart turns away today from the LORD our God, to go and serve the gods of these nations, and that there*

[30] David Chilton, *Days of Vengance* (Dallas, GA: Dominion Press, 1987), 238–239.

> *may not be among you a root bearing bitterness or **wormwood*** (Deuteronomy 29:18 NKJV).

Years later, when the people had indeed turned from Him, God promised through His various prophets to feed the Israelites wormwood, or "water of gall." For example, in Jeremiah 9:15, God declares: *"Behold, I will feed them, this people, with **wormwood**, and give them water of gall to drink"* (Jer. 9:15 NKJV). In other words, He promised that their lives would be bitter and sorrowful because they had rejected Him and betrayed their covenant with Him (see also Jer. 23:15; Lam. 3:15, 19; Amos 5:7). Thus, we can see that when John spoke of a star named Wormwood his original readers would have known that he was talking about the apostasy of Jerusalem and God's coming judgment.

This star named Wormwood also connects to the sixth seal and the stars that fell to the earth (see Rev. 6:13). Once again, the picture introduced in the seven seals becomes clearer in the seven trumpets.

TRUMPET 4: CELESTIAL BODIES DISTURBED

The sun, moon, and stars being affected by the fourth trumpet also echoes back to the sixth seal (see Rev. 6:12–14). Once again, John uses the same language we observed in Matthew 24:29 regarding the destruction of a city or government. In short, celestial disturbances are used as a prophetic idiom throughout the Bible to indicate God's judgment upon a city or nation.

TRUMPET 5: LOCUSTS FROM THE PIT

The fifth trumpet has often confused readers. To understand it, let's think in terms of our painting. This trumpet is like a dark and foreboding corner of the painting that is not well understood. It is so dark and mysterious that one cannot help but stand and stare in wonder. Yet, it has a reasonable explanation. About it, the scholar James Stuart Russell writes:

> With our attention fixed on a single spot of earth, and absolutely shut up to a very brief space of time, it is comparatively easy to read the symbols, and still more satisfactory to mark their perfect correspondence with facts.[31]

In other words, when we keep in mind that these symbols are about the AD 70 destruction of Jerusalem, it becomes easier for us to find the proper interpretation. Many teachers interpret the locusts in this passage as symbols of a modern or future reality, but this contradicts their very claim to take the Bible literally. Harold Eberle and Martin Trench give helpful insight on this in their book *Victorious Eschatology:*

> Some of the most well-known futurist teachers say that these locusts from the bottomless pit are futuristic helicopters that swarm out of the sky and shoot out of their tails a poison that inflicts great pain. Other noted futurists have observed the recent uprising of Islamic terrorists and concluded that the locusts must be the Muslim extremists who will someday attack God's people. These interpretations of the futurists are interesting because these are the same futurist teachers that claim to be taking the Bible literally. If we take those verses literally, then we have to believe that actual locusts with gold crowns, faces like men, hair like women, teeth like lions, and tails like scorpions will swarm across the earth. Furthermore, if the futurist teachers were taking

[31] James Stuart Russell, *The Parousia* (Grand Rapids, MI: Baker Books, 1983), 411.

> the Scriptures literally, they would have to say that their helicopters or their Muslim terrorists were coming out of a bottomless pit. Of course, no futurist could reasonably say that. The idea that futurist Christians take the book of Revelation literally is a myth.[32]

Clearly, the locusts are symbolic, yet not in the way many teachers have suggested. They do not symbolize creatures or vehicles that look like locusts or people who act like locusts. Instead, I believe they symbolize the spiritual reality of first-century Jerusalem and its impending doom. The big picture of this trumpet is a depiction of the demonic state into which Jerusalem had devolved before the Roman destruction.

When the first century Jewish Christians heard John's vision, they most certainly would have connected the locusts to the eighth plague that God had sent upon Egypt at the hand of Moses (see Exod. 10). They would have also noted that the plague was intended for non-Christians and that the Christians were "marked" and protected just as Israel had been during the Egyptian plagues. Essentially, this showed them that Jerusalem had become like Egypt in the eyes of Heaven, and the Christians were enacting a new exodus. This theme of a new exodus of Christians leaving Jerusalem and Judaism is developed much more in the coming sections.

Revelation 11:8 makes it very clear that Jerusalem, *"the city in which our Lord was killed,"* had become *"Sodom and Egypt."* Even here, in the fifth trumpet, we find the eighth plague upon Egypt, but we also find language that mirrors the destruction of Sodom. About the Abyss, it says, *"smoke rose from it like the smoke from a gigantic furnace"* (Rev. 9:2a). This echoes the language used in Genesis to describe Sodom's destruction. When

---

[32] Eberle and Trench, *Victorious Eschatology* (Yakima, WA: Worldcast Publishing, 2006), 155.

Abraham looked toward the city, *"he saw dense smoke rising from the land, like smoke from a furnace"* (Gen. 19:28). It is impossible to escape this conclusion: Jerusalem had turned against God and was now destined for destruction.

Some scholars even believe that the fifth trumpet represents the total demonization of Jerusalem before the destruction by Rome. While this might seem extreme to us, history tells us that the city of Jerusalem had become a very dark and evil place. Josephus, a Jewish historian alive at that time, wrote of how evil Jerusalem had become. Josephus says:

> I am of opinion that had the Romans deferred the punishment of these wretches, either the earth would have opened, and swallowed up the city, or it would have been swept away by a deluge, or have shared in the thunderbolts of the land of Sodom. For it produced a race far more ungodly than those who were thus visited [i.e. more evil than Sodom].[33]

In other words, as a Jew, he looked at his nation's own holy city and declared it so evil that if Rome hadn't destroyed it, surely God would have. Josephus was not a Christian, but as an observer, he recognized the depravity that had taken over Jerusalem and many of the Jews. This may be hard for us to believe. Yet, even Jesus prophesied that Jerusalem and the Jews would become deeply evil in that generation.

> *The men of Nineveh will stand up at the judgment with this generation and condemn it; for they repented at the preaching of Jonah, and now something greater than Jonah is here. The Queen of the South will rise at the judgment with this generation and condemn it; for she came from the ends of the earth to*

[33] Flavius Josephus, *The Jewish War*, Book 5, Section 6.

listen to Solomon's wisdom, and now something greater than Solomon is here.

When an impure spirit comes out of a person, it goes through arid places seeking rest and does not find it. Then it says, "I will return to the house I left." When it arrives, it finds the house unoccupied, swept clean and put in order. Then it goes and takes with it seven other spirits more wicked than itself, and they go in and live there. And the final condition of that person is worse than the first. ***That is how it will be with this wicked generation*** (Matthew 12:41–45).

Here, Jesus was not giving a teaching on deliverance or healing. In context, He was declaring that even though His ministry was cleaning up Jerusalem spiritually, once He was gone, the people would quickly refill Jerusalem with evil, even seven times worse! And that is exactly what happened historically, which is why Josephus gave such a harsh evaluation of Jerusalem. Clearly, the locusts from the pit represent the utter demonization of Jerusalem in preparation for its destruction. While this does not answer every question about every detail in this passage, it is a good starting place and framework for interpreting the details.

TRUMPET 6: FOUR ANGELS AND A BIG NUMBER

The sixth trumpet has two main symbols. First is the command to release the four angels bound at the Euphrates River. When released, these angels (or troops, as it calls them in the same passage) kill a third of the people. In fact, the Roman General Titus had four military legions stationed at the Euphrates that advanced upon and destroyed Jerusalem. In this we see that these angels signify the armies of Rome coming against Jerusalem to destroy and kill.

Second, John uses the mysterious number, *"Twice ten thousand times ten thousand"* to describe the number of the soldiers. Many fanciful explanations have been created regarding this number. Some English Bible translators have simply multiplied it and say the army is 200 million. Yet in this passage, we are dealing with prophetic idioms that are two thousand years old, and we must ask, "What would twice ten thousand times ten thousand have meant to the original readers?" In the Old Testament, *ten thousand* was used to represent an overwhelming and nearly impossible foe. For example, *"Saul has slain his thousands, and David his tens of thousands"* (1 Sam. 18:7, 21:11). So, in this passage, we find John declaring ten thousand times ten thousand and twice over! Basically, he was saying, "Jerusalem, there is no deliverance for you; you are absolutely and unquestionably doomed!"

THE ANGEL AND THE LITTLE SCROLL

Following the sixth trumpet, Revelation 10 and 11 contain a few important asides before the seventh trumpet. First, John encounters an angel who proclaims, *"There will be no more delay!"* (Rev. 10:6). In other words, the judgment foretold in Revelation was about to fall on Jerusalem. Then John hears a voice from Heaven telling him to eat a little scroll that is in the angel's hand. When John asks the angel to give him the scroll, the angel says, *"Take it and eat it. It will turn your stomach sour, but 'in your mouth it will be as sweet as honey'"* (Rev. 10:9). This is an interesting parallel to what happens in Ezekiel 3:1–3, where Ezekiel also receives a scroll that tastes like honey. As we already mentioned, Ezekiel's prophetic message was also about the destruction of Jerusalem, so it is not surprising to find this parallel here. To John's original readers, this would have been a clear indicator of what the prophecy was about. Just as Ezekiel had received a scroll that tasted like honey in his prophetic vision about the destruction of Jerusalem, so too did John. This aside ends with the promise to John that he would prophesy to people, kings, and nations about it (see Rev. 10:11).

THE TWO WITNESSES

The second aside in Revelation 10 tells us about the two witnesses. The two witnesses are the subjects of intense curiosity. For that reason, let's take an in-depth look at the passage in question, starting at Revelation 11:1.

> *I was given a reed like a measuring rod and was told, "Go and measure the temple of God and the altar, with its worshipers. But exclude the outer court; do not measure it, because it has been given to the Gentiles. They will trample on the holy city for 42 months"* (Revelation 11:1–2).

The first important detail here is the fact that the Temple is standing in the vision. When the Temple was destroyed in AD 70, it was comparable to the American Presidential Whitehouse, the Eiffel Tower in Paris, or the Great Pyramid of Giza being destroyed. It was a significant landmark and greatly revered place. This, as mentioned before, is a major clue that Revelation was not written after AD 70, but before. If it was written after AD 70, it makes no sense that John would not ever mention the "past" destruction of Jerusalem and the Temple. Of course, the obvious reason is because it hadn't happened yet. Instead, he was prophesying that it was about to happen.

Also, it's important to note that forty-two months is three and a half years, the exact length of time the siege of Jerusalem took place, from AD 66–70. It was started by the Emperor Nero (the beast) and ended finally under General Titus.

The passage then continues with an introduction of the two witnesses, *"And I will appoint my two witnesses, and they will prophesy for 1,260 days, clothed in sackcloth"* (Rev. 11:3).

We might not realize this if we don't do the math, but 1,260 days is approximately three and a half years. Thus, logically, we can assume that the 1,260 days are the same days that comprise the three and a half years mentioned in the previous verse about the siege of Jerusalem.

The passage then describes the two witnesses using several references to Old Testament passages. First, it says: *They are "the two olive trees" and the two lampstands, and "they stand before the Lord of the earth"* (Rev. 11:4) This is a reference to Zechariah 4:3, 11, 14, where Zechariah prophesies about these very things. Second, it says about the witnesses:

> *If anyone tries to harm them, fire comes from their mouths and devours their enemies. This is how anyone who wants to harm them must die. They have power to shut up the heavens so that it will not rain during the time they are prophesying…* (Revelation 11:5–6).

This is a clear reference to Elijah, who called down fire and stopped the rain for three years. Third, it says of the witnesses, *"…and they have power to turn the waters into blood and to strike the earth with every kind of plague as often as they want"* (Rev. 11:6). This is a clear reference to Moses and the plagues in Exodus 7–11.

In these first six verses of Revelation 11, the timing of this event and the identities of the two witnesses are revealed. We must keep in mind that Revelation is a book full of symbols. This passage is not talking about the actual Moses and Elijah; rather, Moses and Elijah are symbols that represent the Law and the Prophets. With that understanding, we can properly interpret what they do in the remainder of the passage:

> *Now when they have finished their testimony, the beast that comes up from the Abyss will attack them, and overpower and kill them. Their bodies will lie in the public square of the great city—which is figuratively called Sodom and Egypt—where also their Lord was crucified* (Revelation 11:7–8).

Here we observe several interesting details. First, in verse 8, John gives us a huge key to interpreting Revelation when he clearly refers to the "great city" as the city where our *"Lord was crucified."* In other words, he tells us plainly that it is first-century Jerusalem, which is figuratively called Sodom and Egypt. Thus, when we read in Revelation 17 that the whore of Babylon is the great city, we know the whore was Jerusalem, and when we read that Babylon the great city has fallen, we know it speaks of the destruction of Jerusalem. In this way, Revelation 11:8 is a major key to understanding the theme of Revelation—the judgment of first-century Jerusalem and the establishment of the heavenly Jerusalem. Every time we read "the great city," it is a clear reference to Jerusalem (see, for example, Rev. 16:19; 17:18; 18:10–21).

The second interesting detail in this passage is the fact that the two witnesses are killed. The question is, *If the two witnesses represent the Law and the Prophets, how can they be put to death?* I believe the two witnesses (the Old Testament Law and the Prophets) were witnessing about Jesus to the Jews before the AD 70 destruction, but ultimately the Law and the Prophets were ignored, rejected, and "killed" by the Jews. The Law and the Prophets testified as witnesses of Jesus as the Messiah-King. They also testified against Israel, the covenant-breaking nation that stood guilty.

Even Jesus, during His life on earth, referred to the Old Testament as a witness about Him. He said, *"You study the Scriptures diligently because you think that in them you have eternal life. These are the very Scriptures that testify about me"* (John 5:39). Later, after His resurrection, Jesus explained to a few of the disciples on the road to Emmaus how the Old Testament had pointed to Him all along. *"And beginning with Moses and all the Prophets, he explained to them what was said in all the Scriptures concerning himself"* (Luke 24:27). Considering this, I agree with Eberle and Trench's explanation of the two witnesses:

> The Law and the prophets were witnesses against the Jewish people. The Jews had been unfaithful in their covenant with God, and therefore, judgment was coming upon them. However, the Law and the prophets were also the authoritative witnesses of the early Church. As Christians witnessed to the Jews about Jesus Christ, they did not have a New Testament from which to preach. They spoke from the Law and the prophets, convincing many that Jesus was the Christ. Again, we see how the Law and the prophets were sounding throughout the streets of Jerusalem.[34]

This idea is even more fully exemplified in the next two verses in Revelation 11:

> *For three and a half days some from every people, tribe, language and nation will gaze on their bodies and refuse them burial. The inhabitants of the earth will gloat over them and will celebrate by sending each other gifts, because these two prophets had tormented those who live on the earth* (Revelation 11:9–10).

---

[34] Eberle and Trench, *Victorious Eschatology* (Yakima, WA: Worldcast Publishing, 2006), 163.

In other words, the AD 70 world was happy to see Jerusalem destroyed and, with it, all the Old Testament rules, regulations, sacrifices, and ceremonies. As Eberle and Trench put it:

> In what way were the Law and the prophets put to death? When Jerusalem was destroyed by the Roman army, it appeared that everything in which the Jews had put their trust had failed. All had ended. How could they ever rise again? It seemed impossible. While the two witnesses were silent, the people throughout the Gentile world rejoiced because the Law and the prophets also bore witness against them and their sins.
>
> After the dust from Jerusalem's destruction had settled, "the breath of life from God" came back into the two witnesses (Rev. 11:10). The voice of the Law and the prophets rose again. Then the two witnesses were called back into heaven (Rev. 11:12), but at that same time "there was a great earthquake" (Rev. 11:13). As we have discussed before, in apocalyptic language earthquakes represented a demolition or transfer of authority. Indeed, two witnesses were taken to heaven, but the Law and the prophets continued to sound through the Church. The voices of two witnesses were transferred to the Church, and hence, the Law and the prophets continue sounding forth the voice of God even today.[35]

Thus, the testifying, death, and resurrection of the two witnesses symbolize the transition between the old and new covenants. Here is the culmination:

---

[35] Eberle and Trench, *Victorious Eschatology* (Yakima, WA: Worldcast Publishing, 2006), 163–164.

> *But after the three and a half days the breath of life from God entered them, and they stood on their feet, and terror struck those who saw them. Then they heard a loud voice from heaven saying to them, "Come up here." And they went up to heaven in a cloud, while their enemies looked on* (Revelation 11:11–12).

The Kingdom of Jesus revived the Old Testament witness, and instead of a religion full of rules in the earthly Jerusalem, Jesus formed Christianity, enabling His followers to partake of the heavenly Jerusalem.

Many Christians have been taught to read the Book of Revelation with flat literalism rather than as a symbolic book that would have made sense to the original readers. Many have been taught that the Book of Revelation is about our future. This futurist viewpoint offers many interpretations of the two witnesses that are much more fanciful and dramatic than what I have just explained. Those explanations may be exciting, but we must ask ourselves this all-important question: *What was the Holy Spirit actually trying to show John?*

I believe John and the original readers would have clearly and easily seen the two witnesses as representations of Elijah and Moses, the Law and the Prophets, essentially the Old Testament Scriptures. They would have understood that Rome was waging war on the Law-and-Prophets system of Jerusalem and that Rome thought it had killed Judaism. Yet, dead Judaism transformed and resurrected as the heavenly Jerusalem, which is Christianity.

All this culminates in the seventh trumpet.

TRUMPET 7: JESUS WINS

At the seventh trumpet, Jesus is declared the victor, and the ark of the covenant is shown to permanently reside in Heaven. The original ark of the old covenant had gone missing hundreds of years earlier. Now, as John watched this vision, he saw an ark in Heaven! This was not the old ark, but the new ark of the new covenant. Because the new covenant was formed between the Father and the Son, the ark that contains the new covenant resides in Heaven.

Just like the seven seals, the seven trumpets gave a prophetic picture of the judgment that would come upon first-century Jerusalem in AD 70. Though these symbols seems mysterious to us, they were very clear to the early Christians who first read them.

VISION 4: FOLLOWERS OF LAMB OR BEAST

(REVELATION 12:1–15:4)

After John tells about the seals and the trumpets, in this fourth vision, which is the main point of the chiastic arch structure, he approaches the destruction of Jerusalem with a whole new set of pictures. In it, he covers the birth of Jesus, His ascension to the heavenly throne, and the persecution of the Church by Nero (the sea beast) and the Temple rulers (the land beast). Also, he tells of Jesus as the Lamb and the 144,000 Christians on top of Mount Pella avoiding the first century destruction, as well as a great harvest of souls. All of this is covered in Revelation 12–14.

Chapter 12 begins with the woman giving birth. It is no mystery who this woman is—she gives birth to Jesus! Scholars do not debate the identity of her son. In verse 5, it says that He *"will rule all the nations with an iron scepter"* (Rev. 12:5), which is a direct quote of Psalm 2:9 regarding Jesus (see also Ps. 110). Everyone agrees that the son is Jesus. Although some people hold differing opinions as to the identity of the woman, in the big picture it does not matter which of the following interpretations is correct. It does not affect the interpretation of the rest of the visions. Personally, I believe the woman represents the godly remnant of Israel, which Jesus was born from. Yet other commentators have taken this more literally and say she represents the Virgin Mary or Eve the mother of all the living. It is inconsequential to debate this, so we will continue onward.

After the woman brings forth Jesus, He is enthroned in Heaven (see Rev. 12:5), and the woman flees into the wilderness during the three-and-a-half-year destruction of Jerusalem. This she did in obedience to Jesus' instructions in Matthew 24:15–21. According to Josephus, the Christians were safe on Mount Pella during the siege of Jerusalem.

How is this woman both the one who gave birth to Jesus *and* the Church that proceeded from Jesus? As the woman, she represents godly Israel who brought forth Jesus and then also responded to the gospel.

THE BEAST OF THE SEA

Chapter 13 introduces us to the two beasts, the beast of the sea and the beast of the earth. Nothing in Revelation has been subject to as much speculation and misinformation as the beast from the sea. This has been the source of the modern paranoia regarding implanted microchips and barcodes. The type of interpretation that takes place regarding the mysterious number 666 reminds me of the following humorous story:

> Literary scholar Kathryn Lindskoog sent the following to her friends via the Internet to show how almost anyone or anything can be made to read 666.
>
> Given: Barney is a cute purple dinosaur
>
> Prove: Barney is really the Antichrist in disguise
>
> 1. Start with the given: CUTE PURPLE DINOSAUR
>
> 2. Change all the U's to V's (which is proper Latin anyway): CVTE PVRPLE DINOSAVR

3. Extract all Roman Numerals in the phrase: CVVLDIV
4. Convert these into Arabic values: 100 5 50 500 1 5
5. Add the numbers together: 666[36]

To avoid this kind of paranoia and misinterpretation, we must go back to a proper form of interpretation. We must go back to the historical and cultural context and ask, *What would John's original readers have understood this beast to be?* With absolute certainty, I say they would have seen the beast from the sea as Nero (or more generally as the Roman Empire). In fact, this is exactly what the Church taught for most of Church history. Revelation 17:10 mentions another beast in the context of the prophecy about the succession of seven Roman emperors, and because of this, many in the Church historically identified this beast as the Roman Emperor Nero. In my opinion, these are both sensible interpretations.

First, let's talk about the emperor Nero. Nero, who began his reign in AD 54, is famous for being a horrible emperor and deplorable human being. Nero's short life was filled with violence, not only against Christians but also against those closest to him. He murdered several of his family members, including his pregnant wife, whom he brutally kicked to death, and he castrated and "married" a young boy. If that is not bad enough, the historian Suetonius writes about a game that Nero invented, "in which, covered with the skin of some wild animal, he was let loose from a cage and attacked the private parts of men and women, who were bound to stakes."[37]

---

[36] Quoted in Gary DeMar, *Last Days Madness*, 4th ed. (Atlanta, GA: American Vision, 1999), 233.

[37] R.C. Sproul, *The Last Days According to Jesus* (Grand Rapids, MI: Baker Books, 1998), 186–187.

Nero began persecuting Christians in AD 64, after a great fire burned a third of Rome. Many historians believe Nero set this fire, but he blamed it on the Christians and used it as the excuse for his brutal persecution of them. At the age of 31, Nero committed suicide in AD 68, just two years prior to the fall of Jerusalem. Considering all of this, it is not surprising that the early Christians would use a beast to represent Nero. As the historian F.W. Farrar said, "Both Jews and Christians regarded Nero as also having close affinities with the serpent or dragon."[38]

Many writers, both ancient and modern, show us that Nero, a uniquely cruel and evil man, truly was akin to a beast. Kenneth Gentry provides a helpful overview of a few of these sources:

> Tacitus...spoke of Nero's "cruel nature" that "put to death so many innocent men." Roman naturalist Pliny the Elder...described Nero as "the destroyer of the human race" and "the poison of the world." Roman satirist Juvenal...speaks of "Nero's cruel and bloody tyranny." ...Apollonius of Tyana...specifically mentions that Nero was called a "beast": "In my travels, which have been wider than ever man yet accomplished, I have seen many many wild beasts of Arabia and India; but this beast, that is commonly called a Tyrant, I know not how many heads it has, nor if it be crooked of claw, and armed with horrible fangs...And of wild beasts you cannot say that they were ever known to eat their own mother, but Nero has gorged himself on this diet."[39]

Nero clearly fits the bill of the cruel and evil beast. The clearest

[38] W.F. Farrar, *The Early Days of Christianity* (1882), 471–472.

[39] Quoted in R.C. Sproul, *The Last Days According to Jesus* (Grand Rapids, MI: Baker Books, 1998), 186–187.

proof for this interpretation is found in Revelation 17, which says:

> *The beast, which you saw, once was, now is not, and yet will come up out of the Abyss and go to its destruction. The inhabitants of the earth whose names have not been written in the book of life from the creation of the world will be astonished when they see the beast, because it once was, now is not, and yet will come. This calls for a mind with wisdom. The seven heads are seven hills on which the woman sits They are also seven kings.* ***Five have fallen, one is, the other has not yet come;*** *but when he does come, he must remain for only a little while. The beast who once was, and now is not, is an eighth king. He belongs to the seven and is going to his destruction* (Revelation 17:8–11).

As mentioned previously, verse 10, which is speaking of the line of rulers in Rome, tells us exactly how many rulers had already come, which one was currently in power, and that the next one would only last a short while. This perfectly outlines the succession of the Roman Emperors, with Nero as the one who was currently ruling at the time when John wrote the book. Because of this clear description, through much of Church history people have understood the beast in Revelation 17 to refer to Nero.

This is important, because it helps us interpret the beast of the sea that appears in Revelation 13:

> *And I saw a beast coming out of the sea. It had...seven heads.... One of the heads of the beast seemed to have had a fatal wound, but the fatal wound had been healed. The whole world was filled with wonder and followed the beast. People worshiped the dragon because he had given authority to the beast, and they also worshiped the beast and asked, "Who is like the beast? Who can wage war against it?"* (Revelation 13:1–4).

On the Revelation 17 timeline, Nero is the sixth of the seven emperors of Rome (or heads of the beast). After him came Galba, *"the one to come that shall only remain a little while."* The shortness of Galba's reign happened, at least in part, because Rome was faltering as an empire. It had been metaphorically wounded by the horrible reign of Nero. When Nero killed himself in AD 68, Rome's political climate changed dramatically. Nero was the last of the Julio–Claudian line of emperors. At his death, the line ended, and it was, in a sense, like the empire had been beheaded.

In the wake of Nero's sudden death, Rome experienced an event known as the "Year of the Four Emperors." Three short-lived emperors followed Nero (Galba, Otho, and Vitellius). Imagine the tumult that must have shaken the empire during this year! Many people wondered whether the end of the Roman Empire was at hand. It seemed the beast of the Roman Empire had been given a fatal wound. Yet, against all odds, the empire did not collapse. Near the end of AD 69, Vespasian took the throne, and he ruled until AD 80. The beast that had seemed dead experienced a miraculous healing as the empire revived under Vespasian and his son Titus, who established the Flavian dynasty of Roman emperors. This historical event gives us a clear interpretation for the events surrounding the beast of the sea in Revelation 13. The beast who seemed to die and then revived was the Roman Empire and the emperors who ruled it (Nero and those who followed him).

THE BEAST OF THE EARTH

After telling us about the beast from the sea, Revelation 13 tells us about a second beast that came from the earth (see Rev. 13:11–15). The biblical phrase *"the beast from the earth"* is more accurately translated as *"the beast from the land* [*ge*]*,"* which refers to the land of Israel. Rome/Nero was called the beast that arose from the sea because one could see Rome across the sea when standing on the shore near Jerusalem. So, to the Jews, Rome was the beast from across the sea. But another beast also arose closer to home. This second beast arose from within the land of Israel and served the purpose of the beast across the sea.

For the early Christians reading John's vision, the interpretation of this symbol would have been simple. The beast that had arisen in the local region of Jerusalem was symbolic of the Temple rulers, the priestly aristocracy that operated under the power and in the presence of the sea beast as a delegated authority (see Rev. 13:12). Though the Temple rulers should have served the purposes of God, they instead paid homage to the Roman Empire and helped it force its will upon the Jewish people. We see this in the part about the image of the first beast that the second beast gave breath to, as well as the infamous mark of the beast that the second beast enforced on behalf of the first. John described it in this manner:

> *It* [the beast] *also forced all people, great and small, rich and poor, free and slave, to receive a mark on their right hands or on their foreheads, so that they could not buy or sell unless they had the mark, which is the name of the beast or the number of its name* (Revelation 13:16–17).

This mark has been the source of much fear as people have speculated about what it could be. Here, I would like to offer clarity about the mark of the beast, now that we have identified the beast as the Roman Empire. In ancient Rome, the public market was the primary place for buying and selling of goods and services. If people wanted to enter the market, they had to pass through the main gate, where they had to pay homage to the idol of the Emperor. After they did this, ashes were rubbed on their hand or forehead to indicate that they were free to enter the market and conduct business.[40] This was called "taking the mark." This simple explanation demystifies the mark of the beast and gives it a logical historical context.

Along these lines, N.T. Wright points out the significance of the mark of the beast for early believers.

> What's more, worshipping or nor worshipping was quickly becoming the dividing line between people who were acceptable in the community and people who weren't. Not long after this time, some local officials introduced a formal requirement that unless you had offered the required sacrifices you weren't allowed in the market. There were various kinds of marks and visible signs, which were used to set people apart either as 'able to trade' or as 'not able to trade'. From quite early on the Christians were faced with a stark alternative: stay true to the lamb and risk losing your livelihood, the ability to sell or buy; capitulate to the monster, sacrifice to Caesar at the behest of the local officials, and then everything will be all right—except your integrity as one of the lamb's followers.[41]

Richard Anthony confirms this dilemma that faced the early believers, who wanted to stay true to Jesus, but also needed to conduct business in the Roman world.

> The Christians of the first century were under the military authority of Rome, a nation which openly pro-

[40] "Revelation 13:18: Number of the Beast," *The Preterist Archive*, http://preteristarchive.com/BibleStudies/ApocalypseCommentaries/ revelation_13-18.html.

[41] Wright, *Revelation for Everyone*, (Louisville, KY: Westminster John Knox Press, 2011), 121.

> claimed its rulers, the Caesars, to be divine. All those under the jurisdiction of Rome were required by law to publicly proclaim their allegiance to Caesar by burning a pinch of incense and declaring, "Caesar is Lord." Upon compliance with this law, the people were given a papyrus document called a "libellus," which they were required to present when either stopped by the Roman police or attempting to engage in commerce in the Roman marketplace, increasing the difficulty of "buying or selling" without this mark. This is the essence of Scripture's warnings to the early Christians against taking upon themselves the "mark of the beast."[42]

All this makes it clear that the mark of the beast was a first-century commerce law created by a beastly emperor and empire that required all who wanted to buy and sell in the marketplace to offer worship to the emperor. This was true, not only in Rome, but also in Jerusalem, where the second beast served the empire instead of God. Thus, instead of leading people to worship God (as they should have), they caused the Jews to worship the image of the emperor.

The mark of the beast, or the number of its name, is further clarified in the next verse, where John says, *"This calls for wisdom. Let the person who has insight calculate the number of the beast, for it is the number of a man. That number is 666"* (Rev. 13:18). Much hysteria has surrounded this number, yet when we step back and realize that this describes a time in our past, not our future, we can discover a simple interpretation.

To do so, we must first remember that John was expecting his readers to be able to calculate this number and arrive at the same conclusion. John was not writing to readers thousands of

[42] Richard Anthony, "The Mark of the Beast," *Ecclesia.org*, http://www.ecclesia.org/truth/beast.html.

years in the future but to his immediate contemporaries, and he expected them to arrive at the right interpretation. He was not referring to a deep, profound mystery but to natural knowledge when he said, *"this calls for wisdom"* and *"insight* [to] *calculate."* He said this because the number code he used was the ancient Hebrew, not the concurrent Greek language of the day. When the Jewish readers saw what John wrote, they would have mentally translated the numerical value into its corresponding Hebrew letters and spelled out Nrwn Qsr, or as we would pronounce it, Nero Caesar. Some variants of the text say the number is 616 (check the margin of your Bible), which also spells out Nero's name in a secondary manner, further solidifying this interpretation. In other words, this was just another way in which John identified the beast to his first-century readers.

The beast of the sea from Revelation 13 is a symbol of Nero and the Roman Empire that he ruled. The beast of the earth was the Temple rulers of Jerusalem, who forced the will of the first beast upon the Jewish people and led them to worship the Roman emperor's idol.

THE GREAT HARVEST

After John describes these two beasts, in Revelation 14 he sees Jesus (as the Lamb) standing with the Christians (the 144,000) who escaped the destruction of Jerusalem by fleeing to the safety of Mount Pella. At the same time, below the mountain the three angels fly over Jerusalem (Babylon) declaring her destruction below.

Many people have interpreted this passage to speak about an end-time harvest of souls in which billions are swept into the Kingdom of God. I love the idea of a massive wave of salvations, and I believe the Kingdom of God will continue to grow until it fills the whole earth (see Dan. 2; Matt. 13:31–33). However, I do not believe that is what Revelation 14 is about. This is clear in the fact that Revelation 14:17–20 speaks of the harvester angels reaping a harvest that is thrown into the winepress of God's wrath, not into a revival! In other words, in this passage harvest is not a symbol of evangelism.

If we back up and look at a parallel declaration from Jesus, this will begin to make sense. In Matthew 13, Jesus spoke of the approaching harvest. Jesus even indicated it would happen at the end of the age (*aion*), which was at AD 70.

> *The one who sowed the good seed is the Son of Man. The field is the world, and the good seed stands for the people of the kingdom. The weeds are the people of the evil one, and the enemy who sows them is the devil. The harvest is* ***the end of the age****, and the harvesters are angels. As the weeds are pulled up and burned in the fire, so it will be at* ***the end of the age*** (Matthew 13:37–40).

Jesus spoke of good seed and bad seed. Revelation 14:4 speaks of the Christians as the first fruits, the good seed. In Revelation 14:14–20, it speaks of the bad seed being gathered, harvested, and judged. Thus, in neither Matthew 13 nor in Revelation 14 can we find proof for an end-of-the-world harvest of souls! Instead, as with the rest of the book, these chapters foretell the destruction coming upon Jerusalem in AD 70.

The imagery of Revelation 12–14, the central point of the chiasm of Revelation, gives us a whole new dramatic take on the events of the destruction of Jerusalem in AD 70. We read of the woman and her child, the dragon who opposes them, the two beasts who seek to control the people and demand their worship, the Lamb and His faithful followers, and harvester angels who reap the souls of the wicked for judgment. Once again, the overarching theme is the struggle between those who follow Christ and those who do not leading up to the fall of Jerusalem.

VISION 5: THE SEVEN BOWLS OF WRATH

(REVELATION 15:1–16:21)

Revelation 15 marks the beginning of the regression down the other side of the chiastic arch. This regression begins with the seven bowls of wrath. Like the seals and trumpets, the bowls also present a picture of the destruction of Jerusalem in AD 70. It is different from the others, yet it also has many crossovers and parallels.

Though many modern readers tend to jump directly into the symbols of the plagues and want literal interpretations, we must instead back up from the picture in front of us and consider their context. To the first-century Jewish readers, the plagues of Revelation 15–16 would have immediately recalled the only other biblical occurrence of plagues as judgment—Exodus 7–11. In fact, we can find some stunning direct parallels between the two lists of plagues. For example, the second and third bowls are about water turning to blood, which happened to the Nile during the plagues of Egypt (see Exod. 7:20). And the fifth bowl covers the land with darkness just like the ninth plague of Egypt (see Exod. 10:21–29). In Exodus, the Egyptian armies pursued the Hebrews, and the water swallowed them up so the Hebrews were delivered. Yet in the sixth bowl judgment, ironically, an army rises from the river and brings destruction.

In other words, the basic concept in Revelation 15–16 is a clear reversal of the Exodus story. Revelation 11:8 tells us that God saw first-century Jerusalem as being like Egypt and Sodom. Later, we see the Christians make an exodus out of Jerusalem, as represented by the 144,000 who are marked by the Lord (see Rev. 7; 14). Historically, we know that all the Christians fled Jerusalem and found safety in the nearby mountain of Pella, so that no Christians were killed in the destruction of Jerusalem. As the Christians leave, behind them Jerusalem is engulfed in the plagues sent by God. This is the big picture of the bowls. Now Jerusalem has become like Egypt, and God is pouring out plagues upon it.

This may seem like a very challenging idea to those who have never read this passage in this light before. However, I believe the beginning of Revelation 15 makes it very clear:

> *I saw in heaven another great and marvelous sign: seven angels with the seven last plagues—last, because with them God's wrath is completed. And I saw what looked like a sea of glass glowing with fire and, standing beside the sea, those who had been victorious over the beast and its image and over the number of its name. They held harps given them by God and sang the song of God's servant Moses and of the Lamb:*
>
> *"Great and marvelous are your deeds, Lord God Almighty. Just and true are your ways, King of the nations. Who will not fear you, Lord, and bring glory to your name? For you alone are holy. All nations will come and worship before you, for your righteous acts have been revealed"* (Revelation 15:1–4).

Here it's important for us to notice that the Christians sing the song of Moses. This was the song the Hebrews sang right after the Egyptian army was killed in the Red Sea. In Revelation 15, the Christians sing the song of Moses as they are delivered from the new Egypt, first-century Jerusalem. That is what John was conveying to his readers. He goes on:

> *After this I looked, and I saw in heaven the temple—that is, the tabernacle of the covenant law—and it was opened. Out of the temple came the seven angels with the seven plagues. They were dressed in clean, shining linen and wore golden sashes around their chests. Then one of the four living creatures gave to the seven angels seven golden bowls filled with the wrath of God, who lives forever and ever. And the temple was filled with smoke from the glory of God and from his power, and no one could enter the temple until the seven plagues of the seven angels were completed* (Revelation 15:5–8).

The tabernacle of the covenant Law was opened, and out of the Temple came the plagues upon Jerusalem (Egypt). These verses give us the "just cause" for why Jerusalem had become Egypt and deserved the plagues. Their own disastrous disobedience and rebellion toward the covenant Law had brought judgment upon them. If they had accepted Jesus as their Messiah King and His offer of a new covenant, all the curses and plagues of the old covenant would not have fallen upon them.

After John establishes this connection between the plagues against Egypt and the plagues against Jerusalem (the new Egypt), he explains the seven bowls. These are quite repetitive of the seal and trumpet judgments.

In the first bowl, festering sores break out on those who took the mark of Nero. The seven plagues are reminiscent of the plagues upon Egypt in Exodus; thus, this first bowl is a parallel of the sores and boils inflicted on the Egyptians.

In the second and third bowl judgments, first the seas and then the rivers turn to blood. This is an incredibly obvious parallel to the Nile and all the water of Egypt turning into blood at the command of Moses.

In the fourth and fifth bowls, the sun burns the land and the celestial bodies are darkened. Once again, the sun and stars are being affected, which is our continual reminder that John was speaking of the destruction of a city or region. This is also a reverse parallel to the plague of darkness in Exodus. In the fourth bowl, it is the exact opposite; the land receives so much sun that it is burned. Then in the fifth bowl, the skies go dark.

In the sixth bowl, the armies of Rome come from the Euphrates River. We also see mention of Jesus coming in judgment like a thief in the night. In other words, the attack upon Jerusalem would come when no one expected it, and the Christians would need to be alert to escape before the city was surrounded and escape became impossible. Jesus first talks about this in Matthew 24:42–44:

> *Therefore keep watch, because you do not know on what day your Lord will come. But understand this: If the owner of the house had known at what time of night the thief was coming, he would have kept watch and would not have let his house be broken into. So you also must be ready, because the Son of Man will come at an hour when you do not expect him.*

Then Paul also mentions it in First Thessalonians 5:2: *"For you know very well that the day of the Lord will come like a thief in the night."* Peter likewise writes that *"the day of the Lord will come like a thief..."* (2 Pet. 3:10). Then John also includes it in Revelation 3:3, where Jesus says, *"...If you do not wake up, I will come like a thief, and you will not know at what time I will come to you."* He also mentions it in Revelation 16:15, where Jesus says, *"Look, I come like a thief! Blessed is the one who stays awake and remains clothed, so as not to go naked and be shamefully exposed."* I believe these passages refer to the same event. Those first-century listeners needed to live on the edge of their seats and be prepared to run for Mount Pella when the moment of Jesus' coming in destruction came and they saw the armies of Rome surrounding the city.

In the seventh bowl, Jerusalem is divided in three and great hailstones fall. Ancient Jerusalem consisted of three successively higher sections. During the Roman invasion, the Roman army captured the city in three stages, first destroying the lowest section before laying siege to the next section and then finally the third section. In this way, the city was divided into three parts.

The hailstones mentioned in the seventh bowl weighed one talent. Josephus records that the Roman armies lobbed white limestones weighing exactly one talent from their catapults, thus destroying the defenses of Jerusalem in what would have appeared to be a hailstorm of white rocks weighing the exact amount recorded in John's prophecy. Josephus writes:

> The stone missiles weighed a talent and traveled two furlongs or more, and their impact not only on those who were hit first, but also on those behind them, was enormous. At first the Jews kept watch for the stone—for it was white—and its approach was intimated to the eye by its shining surface as well as to the ear by its whizzing sound.[44]

If we keep in mind that the old covenant was the veil and that the removal of the veil was the revealing or revelation of Jesus Christ, then we can look upon this traumatic time—when the old covenant world was being stoned to death for its unfaithfulness to its covenant partner—with gladness that we live fully in

[44] Quoted in David Chilton, *Days of Vengeance* (Dallas, GA: Dominion Press, 1987), 417.

the new covenant. We are in a new covenant of forgiveness that contains no wrath. As Revelation 15:1 says: *"Then I saw another sign in heaven, great and amazing, seven angels with seven plagues, which are the last, for with them the wrath of God is finished"* (ESV).

And Paul writes similarly:

> *For you, brethren, became imitators of the churches of God in Christ Jesus that are in Judea, for you also endured the same sufferings at the hands of your own countrymen, even as they did from* ***the Jews, who both killed the Lord Jesus and the prophets, and drove us out. They are not pleasing to God,*** *but hostile to all men, hindering us from speaking to the Gentiles so that they may be saved;* ***with the result that they always fill up the measure of their sins. But wrath has come upon them to the utmost*** (NASB 1 Thessalonians 2:14–16).

God poured out His wrath upon the old covenant until it was no more, and then He welcomed us into the new covenant of forgiveness, which contains no wrath at all.

VISION 6: THE BABYLONIAN HARLOT

(REVELATION 17–19:21)

After explaining the bowls of wrath, John paints Revelation's most mysterious symbol—Babylon the harlot. Many wild theories have surfaced regarding the harlot, but they have overlooked an incredible clue within the book that will help us interpret the symbols of Sodom, Babylon, and the harlot. That clue is the reoccurring term *the Great City*. In its first occurrence, the text tells us that the Great City is figuratively called Sodom and Egypt, yet literally speaking, this was the city where Jesus was crucified. Therefore, the Great City is Jerusalem. *"Their bodies will lie in the public square of* ***the great city****—which is figuratively called Sodom and Egypt—where also their Lord was crucified"* (Rev. 11:8).

With this key in hand, we can begin to see that Revelation 16–18 speaks of the first century Jerusalem as not only Sodom and Egypt but also as Babylon the great harlot that fornicated with the kings of the earth. After all, the Jews said at Jesus' trial, *"We have no king but Caesar!"* (John 19:15), firmly rejecting their Messiah, their Bridegroom, and joining themselves in adultery with the Roman government.

The idea that Jerusalem the great city (Sodom and Egypt of Revelation 11:8) is the same as Babylon the great city is further reinforced by the chiastic arch structure. Revelation 5–11 is understood by many to depict the destruction of ancient Jerusalem. Therefore, it follows that Revelation 13–18 is the matching picture of the same events on the opposite side of the chiasm.

Some commentators have suggested that both the beast from the sea and Babylon the harlot are Rome. However, this does not seem to be a plausible option for several reasons. While it is clear that the beast from the sea represents Rome, it is also equally clear that the Babylonian harlot city is *not Rome*. Here are three reasons why:

1. The harlot rides the beast (see Rev. 17:3). It does not makes sense that Rome would ride on Rome.
2. The beast hates the harlot and destroys her with fire (see Rev. 17:16). Rome did not hate Rome and destroy Rome with fire.
3. If the beast and the harlot are both Rome, it does not make sense that the beast would wage war on Jesus after the harlot is destroyed. In Revelation 18:21–24 Babylon, the harlot city, is destroyed. Yet, in the next chapter, in Revelation 19:19–21, the beast gathers to wage war against Jesus, but is thrown into the lake of fire.

Interpreting the beast from the sea as Rome is completely reasonable and logical, and most commentators have chosen this interpretation over the course of Church history. But to say that the Great City—Babylon the harlot—is also Rome is unreasonable once we examine the interactions between the beast and the harlot. They absolutely cannot both refer to Rome.[45]

[45] Some commentators, especially Historicists, will make a half leap into Idealism and say that the harlot that rides the beast is the Roman Catholic church, or in more general terms, the "evil spirit or principality of religion." This would mean that the beast [Rome] hated the principality behind Rome, and burned the principality with fire. Then after the principality fell (not because of God, but because Rome cast it down?!), the beast [Rome] was judged separately without an evil principality. This concept falls apart upon thoughtful consideration.

Revelation 17:9 reads: *"The seven heads are seven hills on which the woman* [harlot] *sits."* Yet, the seven hills are not used to identify the Babylonian harlot, but the beast. It is the beast that has seven symbolic heads, which are seven hills. Rome is the city with seven hills in view here. Rome is the beast, and the Babylonian harlot rides on the beast with seven heads, which are seven hills (see Rev. 17:7, 9). Clearly, the harlot and the beast *are two different characters.*[46] Saying that the seven hills surround Rome does not identify the harlot as Rome.

THREE-PARTED CITY

Next, John mentions again (as he did in the seventh bowl of wrath) that the city was divided into three parts. This refers to the fact that ancient Jerusalem was made up of three sections built at different elevations. Thus, the destruction in AD 70 occurred in three parts as the lower to the higher sections were progressively demolished. This is how John words his prophecy of the coming destruction of the great city, Jerusalem, the harlot:

> *The **great city** split into three parts, and the cities of the nations collapsed. God remembered Babylon the Great and gave her the cup filled with the wine of the fury of his wrath* (Revelation 16:19).

The great city is also said to rule over the kings of the earth: *"The woman you saw is the **great city**, which rules over the kings of the earth"* (Rev. 17:18a). Jerusalem's fulfillment of this rulership over the kings of the earth is not obvious unless we consult history, where we discover that it was one of the most important

[46] For an explanation of why Babylon is symbolic of Jerusalem and the beast is symbolic of the Roman Empire, see Kenneth Gentry, *Navigating the Book of Revelation* (Fountain Inn, SC: GoodBirth Ministries, 2009), 141–149.

financial centers of the world at that time. This is also why it is specifically the merchants who mourn its fall in Revelation 18.

> *The merchants of the earth will weep and mourn over her.... They will say, "The fruit you longed for is gone from you. All your luxury and splendor have vanished, never to be recovered." The merchants who sold these things and gained their wealth from her will stand far off, terrified at her torment. They will weep and mourn and cry out: "Woe! Woe to you, great city, dressed in fine linen, purple and scarlet, and glittering with gold, precious stones and pearls! In one hour such great wealth has been brought to ruin!"*
>
> *Every sea captain, and all who travel by ship, the sailors, and all who earn their living from the sea, will stand far off. When they see the smoke of her burning, they will exclaim, "Was there ever a city like this great city?" They will throw dust on their heads, and with weeping and mourning cry out: "Woe! Woe to you, great city, where all who had ships on the sea became rich through her wealth! In one hour she has been brought to ruin!"* (Revelation 18:11–19).

However, the angels and the people of God have a very different reaction to the fall of Jerusalem. Directly following the mourning cries of the merchants and sailors, John tells us what Heaven's perspective is on this event:

> *"Rejoice over her, you heavens! Rejoice, you people of God! Rejoice, apostles and prophets! For God has judged her with the judgment she imposed on you." Then a mighty angel picked up a boulder the size of a large millstone and threw it into the sea, and said: "With such violence the great city of Babylon will be thrown down, never to be found again"* (Revelation 18:20–21).

This dual perspective on the destruction of Jerusalem fascinates me. First, John shows us the human perspective from planet earth in Revelation 18 (mourning over Jerusalem's loss). Then he gives us God's perspective from Heaven at the end of Revelation 18 and into Revelation 19 (rejoicing in the heavens). This was recorded so the Church on earth could know what God's perspective was and not get caught up in the earthly mourning over Jerusalem.

> *After this I heard what sounded like the roar of a great multitude in heaven shouting: "Hallelujah! Salvation and glory and power belong to our God, for true and just are his judgments. He has condemned the great prostitute who corrupted the earth by her adulteries. He has avenged on her the blood of his servants." And again they shouted: "Hallelujah! The smoke from her goes up for ever and ever"* (Revelation 19:1–3).

This was Heaven's perspective on the judgment of Jerusalem. Immediately afterward, John tells us about the great wedding feast between Jesus and His Bride. Revelation is filled with such stark contrasts. One of the strongest is the picture of the Babylonian harlot contrasted against the pure spotless Bride of Christ.

To understand this, we need to know why God referred to Jerusalem as a harlot. The answer is that this image of an unfaithful wife is the picture that God used repeatedly in the Old Testament to describe the unfaithfulness of Israel. Several Old Testament passages use a pattern to describe Israel that is very similar to John's description of the harlot. The pattern goes like this:

1. Israel is God's wife
2. She becomes a harlot
3. She operates in extreme lust

4. She wears fine clothes.
5. Those who prostituted with her begin to hate her, and they come to destroy her.

This pattern is evident in the entire book of Hosea, in Ezekiel 16:15–42 and 23:1–28, in Jeremiah 2:20–3:10, and in Isaiah 1:21; 57:8.[47] The similarity between these Old Testament passages and Revelation 17 is no mistake. The connection is meant to be obvious, and it would have been to John's original readers. They would have immediately understood that he was using the same picture of unfaithful Israel that the Old Testament prophets had used.[48]

It makes sense, then, that John would then describe the Church has the Bride of Christ. As God ends His covenant with His former wife, the unfaithful harlot, He then establishes a new marriage with His pure and spotless Bride. This is imaged in the marriage supper of the Lamb.

MARRIAGE OF THE LAMB

I used to believe the marriage supper of the Lamb was a far distant future event, but our only picture of the timing is in Revelation 19:7, *"Let us rejoice and be glad and give him glory! For the wedding of the Lamb has come, and his bride has made herself ready."* According to this verse, the marriage happened right after Heaven rejoiced over the AD 70 destruction of Jerusalem. It happened right before the beast, the false prophet, and those

[47] I ask the reader to look up and read these passages. For the sake of clarity and space, I cannot quote them in their entirety here.

[48] "The Old Testament uses the metaphor of harlotry exclusively for a city or nation that has abandoned the covenant and turned toward false gods; and with only two exceptions (Samaria in Ezekiel 23:4 and Nineveh in Nahum 3:4), the term is always used for faithless Israel." Martin Trench, email to the author, August 11, 2016.

who took the mark of the beast were all judged in Revelation 19:11–21.

For many, this may require a shift in thinking. The Church is not currently a lonely fiancé withering away and wondering when her wedding will be. The Church is already married to Christ; we are in the new covenant, and we remain in Him, and He remains in us (see John 15:4). In other words, the two have become one, and those who are joined to the Lord are one spirit with Him (see 1 Cor. 6:17).

This means that our modern reality is not necessarily the same as that of the Christians prior to the destruction of Jerusalem. They lived in a unique forty-year transition time between the cross and the destruction of Jerusalem. The new covenant had been established at the cross, but the old covenant still existed. The whole purpose of Jesus' coming in judgment in AD 70 was to completely remove the old covenant and fully establish the new (see Heb. 8:13). When this happened, the Christian reality changed for the better. On the other side of AD 70, we are not looking forward to Christ's coming and the end of the age. We get to live in the current reality of His promises and the fullness of the new covenant.

We are *now* the Bride of Christ. We are not waiting for the marriage supper of the Lamb. We are already married to Him. However, the New Testament believers *were* awaiting their marriage to Christ as part of His coming in AD 70. This becomes clear when we look at several statements in the New Testament and the Revelation sequence of events.

In Ephesians 5, when Paul compares earthly marriage to our union with Christ, he refers to the union of Christ and the Church as *"a profound mystery"* (Eph. 5:32). The two are going to become one. However, in Romans 7:1–6, Paul says a woman cannot be married to another man while her first husband is still alive. This would make her an adulterer. Thus, her first husband must die, and then she will be free to marry the new husband. In saying this, he is illustrating what must happen so that the Church can be married, spiritually, to Christ. The first husband is the old covenant, and the new husband is Christ. So, for the Bride to marry Christ, the old covenant first needed to be done away with.

During the first century, the Church lived as betrothed to her new husband, Christ, but not yet married. In other words, there was a forty-year engagement period. This is why, after the Revelation account of the AD 70 events, John then gives an account of the marriage supper of the Lamb. First the old covenant needed to be fully annulled. Then, the Church could be presented to Christ as His Bride. This is what Paul declared when he wrote, *"Whoever is united with the Lord is one with him in spirit"* (1 Cor. 6:17).

Paul, writing before AD 70, writes as though the marriage has already taken place, as though the Church and Christ have already become one. This is because, in the culture of his day, betrothal was just as binding as marriage.[49] However, the marriage actually happened in the events of Revelation 19. The first mention of the Bride is that she has prepared herself for the marriage: *"Let us rejoice and be glad and give him glory! For the wedding of the Lamb has come, and his bride has made herself ready"* (Rev. 19:7). This comes after the destruction of the Great City Babylon (Jerusalem) by the beast (the Roman Empire) in Revelation 17. The Roman Empire fought against the Jewish people in AD 70, but it also fought against God by persecuting the early Christians. Thus, as Jerusalem faces its destruction, Jesus

[49] "The formal betrothal may take place some years before the marriage. The bridegroom elect sends a present to the girl, the dowry is settled, and if sometime afterwards the engagement be broken off, the young woman, if a Jewess, cannot be married to anyone else without first a paper of divorce from the rabbi." G.M. Mackie, Bible Manners and Customs (Westwood, NJ: Barbour Books, 1991), 131.

calls His followers out from among the hardened Jews of Jerusalem: "'Come out of her, my people,' so that you will not share in her sins, so that you will not receive any of her plagues" (Rev. 18:4). This describes the historical event when the Christians in Jerusalem fled to Mount Pella, where they were spared from the destruction of AD 70.

After the fall of Jerusalem, the time for the marriage supper had finally come. All this is a picture of the union between Christ and the Church that John wrote about prophetically and that Paul stated beforehand, as though it had already taken place. Then, in conjunction with the destruction of Jerusalem and the end of the old covenant, the new covenant marriage supper takes place.[50]

Now, we are on the other side of this marriage supper, and we are the Bride of Christ. The two have become one, and we are equally yoked. We are no longer married to the Law, but we are married to Christ in the new covenant. Because of this, we are now His ambassadors, as co-heirs and co-rulers, to bring the Kingdom into the earth. As those living on the other side of AD 70, with all the inheritance and all the promises, we get to co-make all things new with Christ (see Rev. 21:5). He has overcome, and through Him, we too have overcome. Understanding this changes how we live. It's not just a revelation that certain events are in our past. It changes our understanding of our identity and purpose on earth.

[50] In Matthew 22:1–7, Jesus says, *"The kingdom of heaven is like a king who prepared a wedding banquet for his son. He sent his servants to those who had been invited to the banquet to tell them to come, but they refused to come. Then he sent some more servants and said, 'Tell those who have been invited that I have prepared my dinner: My oxen and fattened cattle have been butchered, and everything is ready. Come to the wedding banquet.' But they paid no attention and went off—one to his field, another to his business. The rest seized his servants, mistreated them and killed them. The king was enraged. He sent his army and destroyed those murderers and burned their city."* Here, verse 7 connects the wedding of the son with the enraged king bringing justice and burning the city. The AD 70 destruction of Jerusalem and the marriage of the Son are unavoidably connected.

VISION 7: THE MILLENNIUM, NEW HEAVEN, AND NEW EARTH

(REVELATION 20–22)

After John's vision of the marriage supper of the Lamb, we find a passage that has been the source of countless debates, divisions, novels, and poor-quality Christian movies.

> *And I saw an angel coming down out of heaven, having the key to the Abyss and holding in his hand a great chain. He seized the dragon, that ancient serpent, who is the devil, or Satan, and bound him for a thousand years. He threw him into the Abyss, and locked and sealed it over him, to keep him from deceiving the nations anymore until the thousand years were ended. After that, he must be set free for a short time* (Revelation 20:1–3).

People have attempted all sorts of wild interpretations of this passage, but I believe the true meaning is much simpler and more straightforward. To begin, we must remind ourselves that Revelation is rife with symbolism. This is essential to understanding the so-called millennium (which just means one thousand years). Nowhere else in Scripture is a thousand-year time period specifically mentioned. In fact, to the Jewish people, the number one thousand simply meant "a whole lot." For example, look at the song in First Samuel 18, *"Saul has slain his thousands, and David his tens of thousands"* (1 Sam. 18:7). This sounds impressive, except that David had only killed Goliath. The Jewish approach to numbers was not the same as the modern literalism we have been taught.

Another example is the claim that God owns the cattle on a thousand hills in Psalm 50:10. Actually, God owns all the cattle on all the hills of the planet, yet to the Jewish reader, using the number *one thousand* was not limiting God's cattle ownership! A third example is in this verse: *"Better is one day in your courts than a thousand elsewhere..."* (Ps. 84:10). If understood literally, this verse would mean 1,001 days elsewhere *would* be better than a day in the house of God. Clearly, that was not the psalmist's message. The point is, based on this precedent, the number *one thousand* used in Revelation 20 does not refer to a literal one thousand years but to a long period of time.

In a recorded sermon, Pastor Bill Johnson of Bethel Church in Redding, California, makes some interesting observations about Revelation 20. He says:

> We have statements in scripture concerning the beasts and the thousand years. For example, it says that the dragon will be bound with chains and cast into a bottomless pit for a thousand years. Now I don't want to take away your millennium... I just want to suggest that we might not know what we are talking about because there are only a couple of verses in the Bible on the subject!
>
> Then Bill Johnson begins to ask questions of the audience:
>
> Bill Johnson: The Dragon, literal or figurative? Is it a real dragon?
>
> Audience replies: Figurative

> Bill Johnson: The Chains, literal or figurative? Is it actual chains?
>
> Audience replies: Figurative
>
> Bill Johnson: The Bottomless pit, literal or figurative?
>
> Audience replies: Figurative
>
> Bill Johnson: The Millennium, literal or figurative?
>
> To this question, the audience replies only with stunned silence.[51]

Bill then goes on to speak about how we have allowed our interpretation of the millennium and other passages to cancel out our responsibility to demonstrate the Kingdom of God in the present—as if many of the Bible's promises are not for today. This point makes all the difference in how we live our Christian lives.

DURING THE MILLENNIUM

Now that we have seen that the millennium symbolizes a long period of time, let's see what John said will happen during the millennium:

> *I saw thrones on which were seated those who had been given authority to judge. And I saw the souls of those who had been beheaded because of their* ***testimony about Jesus and because of the word of God.*** *They had not worshiped the beast or its image and had not received its mark on their foreheads or their hands. They came to life and reigned with Christ a thousand years* (Revelation 20:4).

[51] Bill Johnson, "Mission Possible," CD (15:30 minute mark – 17:05 minute mark).

The English translation of this passage makes it seem like there are two groups of people in view here, yet in the Greek it is clear that John was describing one group of people, the same group from Revelation 6:9–11:

> *When he opened the fifth seal, I saw under the altar the souls of those who had been slain because of the* ***word of God and the testimony*** *they had maintained. They called out in a loud voice, "How long, Sovereign Lord, holy and true, until you judge the inhabitants of the earth and avenge our blood?" Then each of them was given a white robe, and they were told to wait a little longer, until the full number of their fellow servants, their brothers and sisters, were killed just as they had been."*

In chapter 6, we find these martyrs under the throne crying out for justice, but in chapter 20, the same martyrs are given thrones of their own to reign upon! We know this because of the next verse, which says, *"(The rest of the dead did not come to life until the thousand years were ended.) This is the first resurrection"* (Rev. 20:5). This phrase, *"The rest of the dead,"* makes it clear that this group of people is a select number from among the dead. To find out what separates these ones who reign on thrones from "the rest," we need to look at the passage right before chapter 20 begins:

> *But the beast was captured, and with it the false prophet who had performed the signs on its behalf. With these signs he had deluded those who had received the mark of the beast and worshiped its image. The two of them were thrown alive into the fiery lake of burning sulfur.* ***The rest*** *were killed with the sword coming out of the mouth of the rider on the horse, and all the birds gorged themselves on their flesh* (Revelation 19:19–21).

The ones in question, *"The rest of the dead,"* were those who died in the AD 70 destruction, the non-believing Jews. We know this to be true because the time indicator in Revelation 19:20 tells us this happened at the same time as the destruction of the beast and the false prophet, that is Nero and the Jewish rulers.

Here is what we find in Revelation 20:

- A time period that is very long, symbolized by the number *one thousand*
- First-century martyrs sitting on thrones and passing judgment
- First-century Jewish non-believers being judged
- The dragon (devil) being bound in his ability to deceive the nations

Importantly, we have not found any of the following popular ideas:

- A rebuilt Temple in Jerusalem
- The reestablishment of the old covenant system
- Jesus reigning physically upon the earth

These concepts that are not found in Revelation 20 have been injected when teachers take passages from Jeremiah, Zechariah, Ezekiel, and Isaiah and take them out of context to make them fit with Revelation 20.

If I were to simply paraphrase my understanding of Revelation 20, I would explain it this way: The thousand years represents the Kingdom of God. When Jesus came to earth, He bound the devil (the strong man, as in Matthew 12:28–29), and the devil could no longer deceive the nations (see Rev. 20:3). This paved the way for the disciples to disciple all nations (see Matt. 28:18–20). The first century martyrs were given thrones to reign upon in the Kingdom; this occurred in Revelation 11, when Jesus was declared the King over the kingdoms of the earth (see Rev. 11:15) and the first resurrection was indicated (see Rev. 11:17–18). We now live inside the Kingdom of God on the earth, which is growing as the mustard seed and as the leaven going through the loaf (see Matt. 13:31–33). We are in the millennial reign, which is a spiritual Kingdom that is bringing Heaven into the earth progressively (see Matt. 6:10). Someday in the future, the Kingdom will have advanced so far that the only thing remaining to do will be to finally and completely judge the devil. He will be released from his chains to gather up whoever still resists the Kingdom, and the lot of them will be thrown into the lake of fire.

THE MILLENNIUM IS PROPHECY

I do not agree with all the conclusions in James Stuart Russell's work, *The Parousia*. Yet, in it he did an incredible service to theology. Regarding the millennium he gives this great insight:

> The act of binding and shutting up the dragon does indeed come within the "shortly" of the apocalyptic statement, for it is coincident, or nearly so, with the judgment of the harlot and the beast; but the term of the dragon's imprisonment is distinctly stated to be for a thousand years, and thus must necessarily pass entirely beyond the field of vision so strictly and constantly limited by the book itself.[52]

I agree with Russell's interpretation that the dragon (devil) was bound in the bottomless pit in the first century by the work of the cross. Yet by stating this very large number of years (the metaphor *one thousand years*), John passed beyond the immediate AD 70 destruction that, until that point, has been the main

[52] James Stuart Russell, *The Parousia* (Grand Rapids, MI: Baker Books, 1983), 514.

focus of the text of Revelation. In this one instance, we have passed outside the bounds of events shortly to come to pass. Russell continues:

> We believe, however, that this is the solitary example, which the whole book contains of this excursion beyond the limits of "shortly;" and we agree with [the famous commentator] [Moses] Stuart that no reasonable difficulty can be made on account of this single exception to the rule. We shall also find as we proceed that the events referred to as taking place after the termination of the thousand years are predicted as in a prophecy, and not represented as in a vision.[53]

Russell makes a very strong point here; the rest of the Book of Revelation is a visionary experience, yet in this passage, John is not seeing a vision but begins to declare a prophecy. He has moved from operating as a seer with a vision to interpret, and he has started operating as a prophet speaking declaratively regarding the future.

> This act of seizing, chaining, and casting into the abyss is represented as taking place under the eye of the Seer, being introduced by the usual formula, "And I saw." It is an act of contemporaneous, or nearly so, with the judgments executed on the other criminals, the harlot and the beast. This part of the vision, then, falls within the proper limits of apocalyptic vision....[54]

To say it another way, ninety-nine percent of Revelation is a vision with symbols to interpret regarding the destruction of

[53] Ibid., 514.

[54] Ibid., 515.

the old covenant world and the establishment of the new covenant. Yet there is one percent of the Book of Revelation, found in chapter 20, that passes outside the time and space restrictions of the rest of the book and speaks of the distant future. This is clearly shown by the figurative use of the idiom, *one thousand years*.

AFTER THE MILLENNIUM

Most scholars believe several parts of Revelation 20 speak to future events that have not yet been fulfilled. While Revelation is the revealing and unveiling of Jesus Christ and His new covenant—which removed the old covenant veil—the contents of Revelation 20:7–15 *were not* fulfilled in AD 70. This includes Satan's release from prison and his final battle against the people of God, after which he is thrown into the lake of fire. It also includes the great white throne judgement. These two events will happen at the end of the millennium. We do not know how long from now this will be, since the idiom *one thousand* indicates simply a really long time. As the famous Bible scholar, Milton Terry, wrote:

> How long the King of kings will continue His battle against evil and defer the last decisive blow, when satan shall be "loosed for a little time," no man can even approximately judge. It may require a million years.[55]

We live within this unique time in history, the millennium, during which we are partnering with God in His progressive expansion of the Kingdom on earth. This is a truly exciting revelation.

[55] Milton Terry, *Biblical Apocalyptics* (Whitefish, MT: Kessinger Publishing, 2009), 451.

NEW HEAVEN AND NEW EARTH

In the last two chapters of Revelation, we find what many people have understood as a description of Heaven. This is what I grew up believing. I thought Revelation 21–22 described the time after the final judgment. Since then I have realized that these chapters actually describe life within the new covenant.

To understand this, we must first understand some of the terms used in these chapters, particularly *the new heavens and new earth.* These are said to descend out of Heaven: *"coming down out of heaven from God"* (Rev. 21:2, 10). From this, we can gather that there are two heavens, the Heaven where God lives on His throne and the new heaven that descends to the earth. This is clarified further when we see two opposing thoughts about the Temple. The new heaven, which descends to the earth, has no Temple: *"I did not see a temple in the city, because the Lord God Almighty and the Lamb are its temple"* (Rev. 21:22). Yet, the Heaven where God is enthroned does have a Temple:

> *Then God's temple in heaven was opened, and within his temple was seen the ark of his covenant. And there came flashes of lightning, rumblings, peals of thunder, an earthquake and a severe hailstorm* (Revelation 11:19; see also Heb. 9:23–24).

From this, it seems clear that the Book of Revelation speaks about two different heavens, with the Heaven where God dwells being the place of the afterlife. So, we must ask ourselves, how did the first-century reader understand the new heaven and new earth? Was it a figure of speech, or does it speak of literal places? To answer this, we need to start with the basic understanding of *"heaven and earth"* in the first century.

In Matthew 5:18, Jesus says:

For truly I tell you, ***until heaven and earth disappear****, not*

> *the smallest letter, not the least stroke of a pen, will by any means disappear from the Law until everything is accomplished.*

Many of us have read this many times without thinking through the implications of this verse. It gives us a choice between two options. Either heaven and earth still exist and we are under 100 percent of the old covenant Law, or heaven and earth have disappeared, along with the Law. If we understand heaven and earth to be the literal physical earth and heavens (sky), then we must believe that 100 percent of the Mosaic old covenant Law is still in force until the end of this planet. This includes the Temple sacrifices, the three annual pilgrimages to Jerusalem, and many other rules that none of us follow. After all, Jesus said, "… *not the smallest letter, not the least stroke of a pen, will by any means disappear from the Law…"*

Obviously, this does not sit right with most of us, because it violates what we understand about the transition from the old covenant to the new. Alternatively, Jesus could have been using a figure of speech that everyone in the first century understood. This is the only other option for how we can understand this verse. Either Jesus was talking about something else, or the Law is currently 100 percent in effect until the planet is destroyed.

We gain another clue about this puzzle in Jesus' mention of heaven and earth in Matthew 24:35, where He says, *"Heaven and earth will pass away, but My words will not pass away."* Matthew 24 is about the destruction of the Temple in the first century. So, why did Jesus throw add this statement here? The answer would have been obvious to first-century readers, but not so obvious to us. Jews in the first century referred to the Temple system as *heaven and earth.*

Sources as early as Josephus suggest that the very design of the Temple was modeled after the design of heaven and earth:

> ...for if any one do but consider the fabric of the tabernacle, and take a view of the garments of the high priest, and of those vessels which we make use of in our sacred ministration, he will find that our legislator was a divine man, and that we are unjustly reproached by others; for if any one do without prejudice, and with judgment, look upon these things, he will find they were everyone made in way of imitation and representation of the universe. When Moses distinguished the tabernacle into three parts, and allowed two of them to the priests, as a place accessible and common, he denoted the land and the seas, these being of general access to all; but he set apart the third division for God, because heaven is inaccessible to men.[56]

From this, we can gather that *heaven and earth* was a metaphor for the Temple system. According to John Lightfoot, the highly respected author of *A Commentary on the New Testament from the Talmud and Hebraica*, the "passing away of heaven and earth" is the "destruction of Jerusalem and the whole Jewish state...as if the whole frame of this world were to be dissolved."[57]

Maimonides, writing in the 12th century, also confirmed this view of the phrase *heaven and earth*, saying:

> The Arabs likewise [as the Hebrew prophets] say of a person who has met with a serious accident, "His heavens, together with his earth, have been covered"; and when they speak of the approach of a nation's prosperity, they say, "The light of the sun and moon has increased," A

[56] Josephus, *Antiquities of the Jews*, Book 3, Chapter 7.

[57] As quoted in Gary DeMar, *Last Days Madness*, 4th ed. (Atlanta, GA: American Vision, 1999), 192.

> new heaven and a new earth has been created," or they use similar phrases.[58]

If we use this idea to interpret Jesus' words in Matthew 5:18, it suddenly begins to make a lot of sense. Jesus wasn't saying that the Law would hold true until the physical earth was destroyed, but until the metaphorical *heaven and earth*, or the old covenant Temple system was destroyed. It makes sense that when the old covenant ended, the Temple would need to be destroyed along with it, and that is exactly what happened in AD 70. This may seem like a huge shift in thinking, but when we make that shift, we can see that it actually relieves a burden that many Christians have unnecessarily lived under simply because they did not understand the metaphor Jesus used. Charles Spurgeon sums it up well when he says:

> Did you ever regret the absence of the burnt-offering, or the red heifer, or any one of the sacrifices and rites of the Jews? Did you ever pine for the feast of tabernacles, or the dedication? No, because, though these were like the old heavens and earth to the Jewish believers, they have passed away, and we now live under new heavens and a new earth, so far as the dispensation of the divine teaching is concerned. The substance is come, and the shadow has gone: and we do not remember it.[59]

THE FINAL CONSUMMATE ORDER?

Now that we understand the phrase *heaven and earth*, we can see that the new heaven and new earth refer to new covenant

---

[59] Charles H. Spurgeon, *Metropolitan Tabernacle Pulpit*,Vol. 37 (Banner of Truth Publications, 1970), 354.

[58] Maimonides, *The Guide for the Perplexed*, 204.

replacements for the old covenant Temple. Thus, the new heaven and new earth are not a future end-of-the-world reality, but they are a present part of our new covenant experience. Many Christians see the Book of Revelation as an orderly sequence of events leading up to the end of human history, with the introduction of the new heaven and new earth in chapters 21–22. However, now that we know that *heaven and earth* does not refer to the literal heaven and earth, we realize John must have been seeing something else entirely. In fact, when we read closely, we discover that the text itself proves that these chapters cannot be about the afterlife.

The scene described in these chapters contains several imperfections that make it impossible for the new heaven and earth to be the final perfect order of the future world after the final judgment and return of Jesus.

First, in the new heaven and earth, evil people still exist just outside the gates of the city.

> *Blessed are those who wash their robes, that they may have the right to the tree of life and may go through the gates into the city. Outside are the dogs, those who practice magic arts, the sexually immoral, the murderers, the idolaters and everyone who loves and practices falsehood* (Revelation 22:14-15).

Obviously, these sorts of people will not be just outside the gates in eternity, because they will have been judged at the great white throne judgment. Second, it says the leaves of the tree of life are for the healing of the nations, which indicates that the nations have not yet been healed.

> *On each side of the river stood the tree of life, bearing twelve crops of fruit, yielding its fruit every month. And the leaves of the tree are for the healing of the nations* (Revelation 22:2).

Once we reach eternity, there will be no need for healing. All will have already been healed. Third, in the new heaven and earth, nations and monarchies still exist outside the city. *"The nations will walk by its light, and the kings of the earth will bring their splendor into it"* (Rev. 21:24). Once again, this does not fit with our understanding of what it will be like after the final judgment. Fourth, the text says the new Jerusalem will extend 1400 miles above the surface of the earth.

> *The city was laid out like a square, as long as it was wide. He measured the city with the rod and found it to be 12,000 stadia* [approx. 1400 miles or 2253 Kilometers] *in length, and as wide and high as it is long* (Revelation 21:16).

If we try to take this literally, it simply does not make sense. Currently, the world's tallest building stands at 2,722 feet, which is half a mile tall. Planes fly in the Jetstream at 6–7 miles above the earth's surface. Outer space begins at 62 miles above the earth's surface. That means, if we take this passage literally, the new Jerusalem will extend 1,338 miles into outer space. Instead, it is much more sensible to view the new heaven and earth and the new Jerusalem as symbolic for new covenant realities. These final chapters in Revelation do not describe the afterlife, or life after the final judgment, but a reality that is part of our present existence.

Instead, *the new heaven and earth* is a description of new covenant Christianity. Dr. Kenneth Gentry provides the following proofs for this interpretation.

1. Revelation 22:1 speaks of the water of life. This represents God's offer of salvation, which Jesus speaks of in John 4:10–14 and John 7:37. We are invited to come to Him and drink.

2. Revelation 21:14 speaks of the twelve foundations with the apostles' names upon them. Paul also wrote of the Church being built upon the foundation of the apostles and prophets (see Eph. 2:20).
3. Revelation 21:16 speaks of the city as a cube, with each side measuring 12,000 stadia. In modern terms, that is approximately 1,400 miles. Gentry then shows that if one were to measure from Rome to Jerusalem (east to west) and from the northern edge to the southern edge of the Roman Empire, it would add up to 1,400 miles by 1,400 miles, with the isle of Patmos exactly at the center of this measurement.
4. Revelation 21:22 tells us no Temple exists in the new Jerusalem. This is because the work of the cross removed the necessity of the previous Temple.
5. Revelation 21:24 says, *"The nations shall walk by its light."* It refers to Jesus' establishment of the Church as the *"light of the world"* (Matt. 5:14).
6. Revelation 21:25b tells us the gates never close, illustrating the temporal work of ongoing evangelism.[60]

Dr. Gentry then describes the state of gradual growth that characterizes the new creation.

> The principle of gradualism is important to understand as we look into the idea of the present new creation process. Gradualism recognizes that God generally works His will incrementally over time rather than catastrophically all at once. We see this in God's method in the progress of redemption in time (Gen 3:15; Gal 4:4), in Israel's gradual conquest of the Promised Land (Ex 23:29–30; Dt

[60] Kenneth Gentry, *Navigating the Book of Revelation* (Fountain Inn, SC: GoodBirth Ministries, 2009), 180–182.

> 7:22), in God's unfolding of His revelation in history (Isa 28:10; Heb 1:1–2), and in the expansion of Christ's kingdom to the end (Mk 4:26–32; Isa 9:6–7).[61]

I find Revelation 21:5 to fit well with Dr. Gentry's presupposition, *"...I am making all things new...."* Jesus did not declare, *"I have made all things new"* but that there is a process of making all things new. Thus, we should interpret Revelation 21–22 not as a description of a perfected afterlife in the Heaven where God is enthroned, but as the beginning of the "making new" process that started in the first century.

Along these lines, Dr. Gentry provides a beautiful summary of the Book of Revelation:

> In Revelation, John details Christ's judgment upon Israel (Rev 1:7, cp. 3:10) and the collapse of the temple and the old covenant order (Rev 11:1–2, 19). Christianity is born out of Judaism, and for its first forty years functions as a sect of Judaism. But once the temple collapses (Hebrews 8:13; 12:20-28), Christianity is finally and forever freed from its mother and the constraints involved in that previous association (cf. Mk 2:21–22; Jn 4:20–24). John is picturing the glory of new covenant Christianity, which arises from the ashes of collapsed Judaism (cp. Mt 8:11–12; 21:43; 22:1–10). Christ promises victory over Israel and her resistance: "Truly I say to you, that you who have followed Me, in the regeneration when the Son of Man will sit on His Glorious throne, you also shall sit upon twelve thrones, judging the twelve tribes of Israel" (Mt 19:28).[62]

---

[61] Ibid., 182.

[62] Ibid., 184.

Although Revelation may give us some clues about what Heaven is like, Revelation 21 and 22 are primarily concerned with describing the new covenant world that replaced the old covenant world. The new covenant was inaugurated at the cross and fully established at the marriage supper of the Lamb. Now the new covenant age continues on as we co-labor with Christ to make all things new and to advance His Kingdom influence in this earth.

The ultimate goal that we continue to work toward until Jesus returns is found in Ephesians 1:9–10:

> *...making known to us the mystery of his will, according to his purpose, which he set forth in Christ as a plan for the fullness of time,* ***to unite all things in him, things in heaven and things on earth.***

One day, after the Kingdom has fully grown (see Matt. 13:31–33) and all things have been made new (see Rev. 21:5), God's will shall be done on earth as it is in Heaven, and all things in Heaven and on earth will be in unity (see Eph. 1:10).

THE EPILOGUE
(REVELATION 22:12–21)

Like the introduction, the epilogue to Revelation provides a beautiful frame to the contents of the book. As we did with the introduction, we will look briefly at the text of the epilogue to see how it frames the rest of the book. The epilogue begins with this statement:

> *Look,* ***I am coming soon!*** *My reward is with me, and I will give to each person according to what they have done. I am the Alpha and the Omega, the First and the Last, the Beginning and the End* (Revelation 22:12–13).

At both the beginning and the end of Revelation, we find declarations of the timing of the events prophesied in the book. When Napoleon Bonaparte wrote that he would attack *soon,* he didn't mean in *our* future. When Abraham Lincoln wrote of ending slavery *soon,* he wasn't referring to our future. So why would we think Jesus was talking about *our* future when He said *soon*? Only by disrespecting the text can we reinterpret soon to mean not *soon*. The destruction of Jerusalem was soon for the original readers of Revelation, and Jesus was exactly right in saying it would happen soon. He then continues by reminding His readers of their two choices:

> *Blessed are those who wash their robes, that they may have the right to* ***the tree of life and may go through the gates into the city.*** *Outside are the dogs, those who practice magic arts, the sexually immoral, the murderers, the idolaters and everyone who loves and practices falsehood* (Revelation 22:14–15).

In the first century, individuals had two choices. They had two Jerusalems to pick from (see Gal. 4:24–26; Heb. 12:22; 13:14). If they accepted Jesus as their Lord and Messiah, they spiritually went through the gates and entered into the heavenly Jerusalem, that is, the Bride of Christ, the Church. In contrast, if they chose not to partake in the heavenly Jerusalem, by default they chose the earthly Jerusalem, which was filled with evil and about to be judged. This is a summary of the whole message of the book. Then Jesus reassures His faithful followers that their wait has not been for nothing.

> *I, Jesus, have sent my angel to give you this testimony* ***for the churches****. I am the Root and the Offspring of David, and the bright Morning Star* (Revelation 22:16).

The churches had experienced nearly forty years of incredible persecution since Jesus had left, and it was time for an update from Heaven. As Jerusalem stood on the eve of incredible tragedy, Jesus gave an update to His followers on earth and encouraged them that He had not forgotten His promise to come. He ends with a powerful anthem of His coming and a warning to any who would alter His prophecy:

> *The Spirit and the bride say, "Come!" And let the one who hears say, "Come!" Let the one who is thirsty come; and let the one who wishes take the free gift of the water of life.*
>
> *I warn everyone who hears the words of the prophecy of this scroll:* ***If anyone adds*** *anything to them, God will add to that*

> *person the plagues described in this scroll. And* ***if anyone takes words away*** *from this scroll of prophecy, God will take away from that person any share in the tree of life and in the Holy City, which are described in this scroll.*
>
> *He who testifies to these things says, "Yes,* ***I am coming soon.****" Amen. Come, Lord Jesus. The grace of the Lord Jesus be with God's people. Amen* **(Revelation 22:17–21).**

Some have wondered why Jesus inserts this warning in verses 18 and 19. My simple thought is this: If people in the first century changed the context and content of this prophecy regarding the impending destruction of Jerusalem (see verse 20), others could easily misinterpret and misunderstand the text. That would result in Christians being trapped inside Jerusalem during the destruction. It was imperative for the whole content of Revelation to remain intact, because it was Jesus' directions to the churches in the first century for how to avoid the destruction.[63]

According to Albert Barnes, "Not one Christian perished in the destruction of that city [Jerusalem]."[64] Therefore, we know that every Christian in the first century understood the Olivet discourse and the Book of Revelation. Since they knew the passages were about their near future, they knew when to flee to the nearby mountains. The Book of Revelation was an invaluable blessing in the first century, but as time passed and the events of the first century and AD 70 faded into the distant past, people ceased to understand Revelation's purpose for those living right before the AD 70 destruction. What seems like

[63] In chapter 3, "Naming the Work," I also noted a parallel between Revelation 22:17–21 and Deuteronomy 4:2. In both cases, these passages are typical of historical covenant treaties, thus pointing to the fact that Revelation is a book about covenant.

[64] Albert Barnes, *Barnes' Notes on the New Testament* (1832), Matthew 24.

a mysterious book to us was actually a clear directive for them. When we understand that, we can look back with awe at what God did for His people, and we can look forward with hope for our future.

CONCLUSION

IS REVELATION STILL RELEVANT?

Many untrained students have stood in front of a work of art and asked themselves, *Does paint smeared on a canvas really have any continuing value or relevance?* To the untrained, it does not. Instead, it is just a mess and a mystery. The same is true of the Book of Revelation. But for students trained in art history, the art before them has incalculable value because the artist, the context, the purpose, the location, and the timeframe all tell a story—a story worth understanding and recording.

In response to what we've discussed in this book, some may wonder whether Revelation still holds value for modern readers. For many, this is a troubling idea. In fact, Watchman Nee used that same question as an argument against this particular view of Revelation when he wrote:

> The period when Revelation was written constitutes a serious problem, in part because some Rationalistic teachers have advocated an earlier date for its composition—they assert that probably it was at the time of the reign of the Roman Emperor Nero. They have formulated this particular time frame in order to establish the theory that the serious proclamations recorded in the book of Revelation were all fulfilled after the infamous and

> devastating fire that took place in Rome in Nero's time. According to this theory, what the book prophesied actually pointed only to the persecutions of the Christians of old and destruction of Jerusalem together with events, which occurred at that very period of Roman History. The prophecy concerning the beast or the Antichrist simply has reference to the tyranny and evil deeds, which were perpetrated by Caesar Nero. And thus the contents of the entire book have been completely fulfilled by the events, which occurred around the time of Nero. For these advocates, Revelation is now only a book of already fulfilled prophecies. And hence it has no future spiritual value for us Christians. It merely forms a special part of Roman history and / or ancient Church History. But if that is true, then will not Revelation be quite a meaningless book for us Christians today?[65]

Here we see that, according to Nee's perspective, to understand Revelation from this point of view is to remove all lasting value or purpose. I disagree. If I could dialogue with Nee, this is what I would say:

According to your logic, how does the Old Testament have lasting value? It was written about events that have already occurred! How does the story of the first Christmas have lasting value? It was written about events that have already occurred! How does the gospel record have lasting value? It was written about the events of Jesus' life that have already occurred! How does the story of the crucifixion have lasting value? It was written about events that have already occurred! How do the letters of Paul, Peter, James, and John have lasting value? They were written to Christians who have long since died!

[65] Watchman Nee, *Aids to Revelation* (Fort Washington, PA: Christian Literature Crusade, 1983), 17–18.

The fact is, the entire Bible has continuing value and relevance, regardless of whether or not particular passages are about past events! The fact that Revelation is not a mysterious jigsaw puzzle to be fiddled about and dissected by each generation does not mean it has less relevance.

Rather, from Revelation we learn many things of value. Here are five of the most significant lessons we can learn from Revelation *despite* the fact that it does not prophecy events in our future:

1. We have been fully established in the new covenant with our bridegroom, King Jesus.
2. All wrath has been poured out on the old covenant system and never has to be repeated.
3. We are working with the King to *make all things new.*
4. There is no reason to fear a future one-world government run by the beast.
5. Jerusalem is not to be an idol for the modern Christian.

Now that we clearly see *The Art of Revelation*—the total removal of the old covenant and the beautiful display of the new covenant that we live in—it's time to get back to work and make all things new.

The Welton Academy Supernatural Bible School Online is neither a supernatural ministry school nor a dusty seminary. We have created a unique program that teaches the depths of the Word without becoming boring or denying the supernatural. We are focused on teaching the Bible through a New Covenant Kingdom perspective.

It is our passion to see all Christians operate in the supernatural, know their identity, walk in freedom, and be powerful people. We are not simply aiming at creating pastors and missionaries. No matter what your calling is, you must have a firm foundation in your identity, freedom, and the supernatural. We think long-term and build powerful people.

To be a part of where the Lord is leading the Church in the years to come, we must lay a new foundation in our understanding of the Word. The Word hasn't changed, but some of our understanding of it must change; otherwise, we will hinder our growth and the advancement of the Kingdom of God.

A powerful advantage of the SBS is that while you are spiritually growing you are not isolated. You have the opportunity to interact with others who are growing in the same deep things you are learning. You are joining a movement with others who are pressing forward with God.

Go to www.weltonacademy.com for registration
and more information.

Additional Material by Dr. Jonathan Welton

UNDERSTANDING THE WHOLE BIBLE

The King, The Kingdom, and the New Covenant

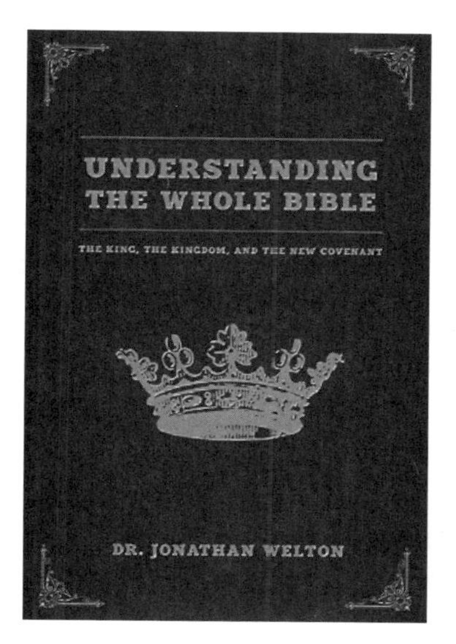

This textbook is the distillation of a nineteen-week course, Understanding the Whole Bible from Genesis to Revelation taught by author and theologian Dr. Jonathan Welton. If you want to devour the Word, this textbook will give you the knife, fork and even tuck in your napkin and teach you how to eat! Topics include: - Learn the difference between Systematic and Biblical Theology - How did we get our Bible? - Translations and study tools - Freewill versus Predestination - Dispensationalism and Covenant Theology - Cessationism and Supernaturalism - The Five Major Covenants: Noah, Abraham, Moses, David, and the New Covenant - The Covenant Promises fulfilled - God is not an Old Covenant monster - Understanding the At-One-Ment - Better Covenant Theology - The Great Covenant Transition - The End of Age - The Unveiling of Jesus - The One Law of the New Covenant World.

What others have said:

This is an instant classic. 'A book that shows the Bible is the story of God's covenant journey with His people.' Dr. Jonathan Welton has presented one of the most comprehensive and revelatory books on the King, the Kingdom, and the New Covenant.

Jonathan Welton has shifted my entire understanding of the Bible and his book provides so much clarity on what the Bible really is saying. Seeing Scripture through the lens of the covenants is so needed and many miss this vital perspective.

Understanding the Seven Churches of Revelation

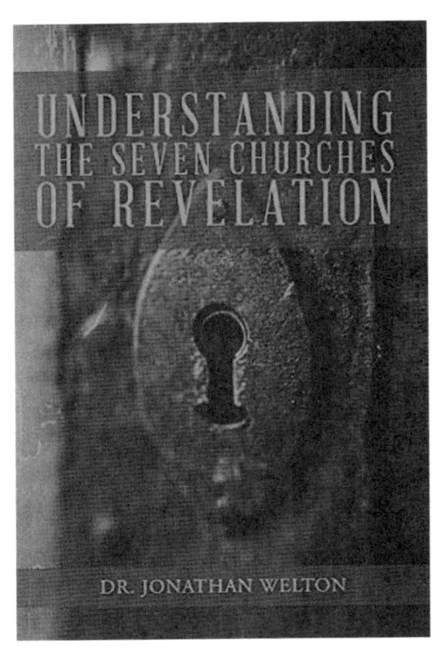

What little has been written about the seven letters to the churches in Revelation tends to utilize the lens of interpretation called dispensationalism. But the book itself gives us no indication that the letters to the churches are anything but letters to churches in the first century. In this unique book, Jonathan Welton applies the historical-contextual method of hermeneutics to these letters, which begins with the questions *who, where, when, what*, and *why*.

Jonathan delves deeply into the historical context of each individual letter for excellent, but often hidden insight. Since Church history tells is that each of these churches was a literal historical church (not a metaphor, as dispensationalism proposes) John was addressing specific situations relevant to each church during the first century. When we look at the historical and cultural dynamics of the cities, we find that the letters are, in fact, very specific and unique to the historic reality.

Says the author:
"I have read other historically thorough sources, and I have done my own research, including traveling to and touring the modern locations of each of the seven churches mentioned in chapters 2 and 3 of the book of Revelation. In doing so, I have discovered an incredible list of connections between the cultural, geographical and historical events of the first century in these cities and the contents of Jesus' letters to them. I've written the book I wish I had read when I was seventeen and eager to understand what these beautiful yet cryptic letters were all about. I believe these letters hold significant and relevant information that influences our understanding of this book as a whole and that holds practical relevance for our lives."

New Age Masquerade

By far this is the most unique book regarding the New Age Movement from a Christian Perspective. Jonathan Welton reveals the history of the New Age Movement from Swedenborgism to the Modern New Age, while demonstrating that each of the movements leaders originally had roots within Christianity. The New Age isn't a Christian movement, but it is a movement away from a Christian foundation.

Other Topics covered:

- What is the difference between a Christian and a New Ager"
- Are we to have showdowns like Elijah vs the Prophets of Baal?
- How do we discern the counterfeit from the authentic?

Are you curious about what the Bible says about: The Age of Aquarius, the silver cord, necromancy, the Zodiac, ESP, Automatic writing, ectoplasm, and zombies? This book is for you!

From the Foreword by Patricia King

"Jonathan Welton has done a tremendous job writing New Age Masquerade. In it, he brilliantly discloses the biblical foundations that have been counterfeited in specific New Age Practices. The enemy has take scriptural truth, twisted it, and dangled it before the spiritually hungry. He knows all people were created for encounter with God, and his goal is to draw people away from Jesus and unto himself.
"Remember, if there is a counterfeit, there must be an authentic. In New Age Masquerade, Jonathan will introduce you to the authentic."

Additional Material by Dr. Jonathan Welton

RAPTURELESS
Third Edition

In 2012, the best-selling author and founder of Welton Academy, after ten years of thorough research, released the first edition of Raptureless. It has gone viral and has sent a shockwave through the Charismatic/Pentecostal church world. Dr. Welton's writing gift has made Raptureless one of the easiest to read yet deepest quality books on the subject of the endtimes. He proves beyond a shadow of a doubt that the Great Tribulation is an event, which occurred in the First Century. Without complicated wording, he demonstrates that the AntiChrist is not a person in our future, and that we are not waiting for Jesus to be enthroned in Jerusalem. Basically, this book is the opposite of everything you thought you knew about the endtimes, simply written and thoroughly, historically proven. Now available in it's third edition, with new editing and chapter reordering, as well as 60% more content than the original.

What others have said:
"Jonathan Welton has taken a bold step in confronting one of the greatest 'sacred cows' of our day: end time theology! The fear created by the expectation of a coming antichrist and a great tribulation are keeping many believers in bondage. Many believe that defeat is the future destiny of the Church. In his easy to read presentation, Jonathan dismantles many of the popular ideas in the Church about the end times." ~ *Joe McIntyre*

ADDITIONAL MATERIAL BY JONATHAN WELTON

The School of the Seers by Jonathan Welton

Your how-to guide into the spirit realm!

The School of the Seers is more than a compilation of anecdotal stories. It is the how-to guide for seeing into the spirit realm.

The fresh, profound, and new concepts taught in this book take a mystical subject (seers and the spirit realm) and make them relevant for everyday life.This book takes some of the difficult material presented in other seer books and makes it easy to understand, removes the spookiness, and provides practical application of a dimension that is biblically based and scripturally sound. Get ready to enter the world of a seer! In this groundbreaking and revelatory book, Jonathan Welton describes his unique journey in which God opened his spiritual eyes. He shares how you too can activate this gift in your life.

Discover the keys from Scripture that will help you:

- See with your spiritual eyes.
- Use the four keys to greater experiences.
- Recognize what may be hindering your discernment.
- Learn about the four spirits.
- Access divine secrets and steward heavenly revelation.
- Learn how to really worship in Spirit and in Truth.
- Understand meditation, impartation, and so much more...

ADDITIONAL MATERIAL BY JONATHAN WELTON

Eyes of Honor: Training for Purity and Righteousness
by Jonathan Welton

After struggling with sexual temptation for years, author Jonathan Welton devoted himself to finding a way to be completely free from sexual sin. He read books, attended 12-step groups, and participated in counseling—with no success.

Spurred on by countless friends and acquaintances who shared a similar broken struggle and longed for freedom, the author searched Scripture. There he found the answer, which he shares with you in a compassionate, nonjudgmental way.

Eyes of Honor helps you understand how to live a life of purity by realizing:

- Your personal identity
- How to view the opposite sex correctly
- Who your enemies are

Eyes of Honor is honest and refreshing, offering hope and complete freedom and deliverance from sexual sin. Jesus' sacrifice on the cross and your salvation guarantee rescue from the appetite of sin. Your true identity empowers you to stop agreeing with lies of the enemy that ensnare you.

"This book is stunningly profound. He got my attention and kept it." ~ **Dr. John Roddam**, St. Luke's Episcopal

"Jonathan has written one of the best books on being free from bondage by dealing with the root issues of sin. I highly recommend reading this book.
~ **Dr. Che Ahn,** Chancellor Wagner Leadership

ADDITIONAL MATERIAL BY JONATHAN WELTON

Normal Christianity: If Jesus is Normal, what is the Church? by Jonathan Welton

Jesus and the Book of Acts are the standard of *Normal Christianity.*

Remember the fad a few years ago when people wore bracelets reminding them, What Would Jesus Do? Christians state that Jesus is the example of how to live, yet this has been limited in many cases to how we view our moral character. When Christians tell me they want to live like Jesus, I like to ask if they have multiplied food, healed the sick, walked on water, raised the dead, paid their taxes with fish money, calmed storms, and so forth. I typically receive bewildered looks, but that is what it is like to live like Jesus!

Perhaps we are ignoring a large portion of what living like Jesus really includes. Many Christians believe they can live like Jesus without ever operating in the supernatural. After reading in the Bible about all the miracles He performed, does that sound right to you? (Excerpt from book)

What others have said

I believe before Jesus returns there will be two churches. One will be religious, and the other will be normal. This book of Jonathan Welton's will help restore your childlike faith, and you will become normal!

~ **Sid Roth,** Host of It's Supernatural! Television Program